THE HOPES

OF

HOPE CASTLE;

OR,

THE TIMES OF KNOX

AND

QUEEN MARY STUART.

BY MRS. S. T. MARTYN,

AUTHOR OF "THE WOMEN OF THE BIBLE," "ALLAN CAMERON," ETC.

AMERICAN TRACT SOCIETY,
150 NASSAU-STREET, NEW YORK.

The principal characters and facts here presented are veritable history.

CONTENTS.

THE

HOPES OF HOPE CASTLE.

I.

Coming Home.

"Breathes there a man with soul so dead,
Who never to himself hath said,
This is my own, my native land?
Whose heart within him ne'er hath burned
As home his footsteps he hath turned
From wandering on a foreign strand?"

JOURNAL KEPT BY KATHIE HOPE FOR HER FRIEND LADY ELLEN MAXWELL.

HOPE CASTLE, June, 1558.

WHEN I bade farewell to France, I promised the dearest friend I left behind that I would keep a faithful journal of the daily events of my life, and the feelings of my own heart, and forward it to her from time to time as I might have opportunity. In my sorrow at parting, I would have promised a much more difficult thing, had it been required of me, without hesitation; and now the pledge must be fulfilled, though I may have little of interest or importance to write.

After an absence of six years I am once more among my kindred and friends, in the bosom of my family. But this is not my childhood's home, the dear old Edinburgh home, in the dark and close wynd, where the sunlight visited us rarely and by stealth, and my only ideas of green fields and waving forests were taken from Calton hill and St. Leonard's crags. But yet, notwithstanding its gloomy surroundings, there are none but bright and pleasant recollections connected with the old house, for every room is lighted up with memories of the love and kindness that made my childhood so happy.

When at twelve years of age I was

sent to the convent in France for education, my young heart was ready to break with loneliness and grief. Shall I ever forget whose goodness it was that first comforted me, and made me feel that, even among strangers in a strange land, a sister friend was watching over me? I am not naturally demonstrative, and often when I feel most can say least. She may have thought me cold and unfeeling, but if she could see my heart, it would there be found that all her thousand acts of kindness are graven as with the point of a diamond, never to be effaced. As a whole, I cannot say that my recollections of convent life are very delightful; but this only makes the image of the one kind friend who was guardian, counsellor, sister—all dear names in one—stand out the more brightly in my memory. What one like Lady Ellen could have seen to call forth her love, in an ignorant, unformed Scotch lassie, as I must have seemed to her, educated as she had been in the polished French court, I know not; I only know that it seemed to me as if one of the angels about whom we read had become visible for my benefit; and this thought gave me courage to try to become all that this beloved friend wished me to be.

But I have wandered far from my starting place, and can almost see the quiet smile with which my friend will say to herself, "It would not be Kathie were it otherwise."

Here I am in our grand ancestral castle, on the banks of the Tay, near the goodly old city of Perth, and surrounded by scenery which cannot be surpassed even in Scotland, the home of the sublime and beautiful. The castle is an immense irregular pile of buildings, full of concealed passages, winding stairways, mysterious chambers, and rooms hallowed by great historic events. The portraits of stern warriors and knights frown upon me from the canvas when I walk through the picture gallery, making me feel like a very degenerate scion of their ancient line, as I steal along after nightfall, afraid of my own shadow, and trembling at the sound of my own footsteps.

None but those who know the strictness and privations of convent life can imagine the delight with which I roam at will through the various apartments of the castle, musing on the glories of the past and weaving bright plans for the future; or lose myself in the beautiful grounds, where one is at a loss which most to admire, the wild grace of nature or the skill with which art has adopted and carried out her plans. The magnificent forest trees which interlace far above head, forming an arch grand and solemn as some cathedral aisle; the embowered walks, leading at every turn into some new scene of beauty; the sylvan lake, on whose bosom the sunlight falls through intervening foliage, making it sparkle like a diamond set in emeralds; all these, to one who has hitherto known nothing but the garden of the convent, are a never-failing source of interest and delight.

I have chosen for my own a room in the highest turret of the Astrologer's tower; so called from an ancestor who went mad in the pursuit of the philosopher's stone. In the evening I often fancy I hear strange noises in the rooms below, where his unhallowed experiments were carried on, or a slow step painfully ascending the stairs that lead to the closed laboratory. But one glance from my window puts all such fancies to flight. I wish I could adequately describe the glorious prospect that meets my eye as I look abroad. The silver Tay, winding about among the beautiful Perth Inches, as if unable to leave a scene so lovely; far away to the north the stately Grampian mountains; while just across the river the Perthshire hills are grouped together in picturesque confusion, the fair city nestled in a bend of the stream, and over all the blue sky of my native land bending lovingly, as if to frame the picture.

Oh yes, my home is all that one could wish; but shall I confess it to my own heart, that in the midst of it all I am ill at ease and far from happy? It may be that I am fanciful and wayward, and gladly would I believe myself so were it possible. But I am disturbed with a strange and increasing fear that these friends of mine, so generous and kind, are not one with me in our holy faith; in a word, that the fearful heresy about which we heard so much in the convent has been at work here, perverting and ruining souls. My father and brother have been away from home much of the time since my return, so that they are still comparative strangers, though I know that they are regarded as among the leaders of the congregation, as the reformed church is usually styled. My excellent mother is gentle and tender as ever, and carefully avoids every thing that can lead to controversy between us; but I cannot help seeing that she is greatly changed; and darling Jessie, my sweet young sister, looks upon me with pity and sorrow in her dove-like eyes, whenever she sees me engaged in acts of worship or penance. What is to be the end of all this?

It is sufficiently painful to differ from those one loves in matters pertaining to this world only, but when the safety of the soul is at stake it is hard to reason calmly on the subject. I was not prepared, from all I had heard in France, to realize the complete revolution which has taken place in public opinion throughout this land. The Protestant faith is now the established religion of the realm, and Catholics find themselves barely tolerated where once they have reigned supreme.

II.

Heresy in the Household.

"If I had loved thee better than my life,
Though thou wert needful to me as an eye,
Or hand, or foot, yet tainted so
With this foul heresy, I'd cast thee off,
If my heart's blood went with thee."

JULY.

LAST evening Jessie came suddenly into my room, and found me employed in telling my beads. When the rosary was finished, she threw her arms about my neck, and with tears in her eyes, exclaimed:

"Kathie dear, of what use is it to repeat those Latin prayers to men and women of whom you know nothing, except that they were, if indeed they ever lived at all, only frail mortals like yourself?"

"Of what use?" I repeated; "why, Jessie, don't you believe in saying prayers?"

"I believe, dear sister," she replied with sweet seriousness, "in praying to God through his son Jesus Christ, for what we need, but not in repeating words in a dead language, whose meaning we cannot understand. I believe too, that since our heavenly Father gives us the privilege of coming directly to himself with our wants, we need not and ought not to seek the mediation of those who, however holy, can have no strength or goodness to impart to others. 'There is none other name under heaven given among men, whereby we must be saved;' and since this is so, why should we look anywhere else but to Him?"

"Oh, Jessie," I could not help exclaiming; "what is it that has come between us? I believe and practise only what I have been taught; but you--you are fearfully changed. Can this be the heresy of which the holy fathers warned us so often? Nothing around me seems the same as formerly; even you, my sweet play-fellow and sister, no longer sympathize with me in my dearest interests. I tremble for the safety of those I love best on earth."

"Dearest Kathie," she replied with touching humility, "I am only an ignorant young girl, and know far less than you do; but I cannot believe that loving and trusting the blessed Saviour with my whole heart can ever lead me into dangerous heresy. He says in his blessed word, 'Him that cometh to me I will in no wise cast out.' Can it be wrong, my sister, for a poor sinner like me to take him at his word?"

"Holy mother of God, protect me," I exclaimed; "for though I know and feel that you are wrong, I have no arguments by which to expose your error."

"But we may love each other just the same, may we not, dear sister, even while we are unable to see alike on this subject? If we could only read the Bible together, I am sure it would lead us both into all truth."

I was so shocked at this proposal, that I replied, perhaps too hastily,

"Never, Jessie, never will I peril my soul by reading a book which is expressly forbidden by our church to the unlearned; and I shall pray constantly to the Madonna that you may be brought to see your fatal error before it is too late."

She made no reply, but kissing me tenderly, soon after left the room, and the subject has not been renewed between us since. But I have seen and heard enough to know that a great gulf is opened between me and the rest of my dear family, across which I can never pass to them, and which I fear will separate us for ever.

The conversation between Jessie and myself has brought to mind a circumstance that occurred during my voyage home, and which until now I had forgotten. The gentleman who was to have accompanied me, found at the last moment that he must be detained still longer in Paris, and accordingly introduced me to a friend of his, who was going to Scotland in the same vessel with myself. He placed me under his care, saying pleasantly, "This young lady is a true daughter of the church, Fraser, and I trust you will not infect her with any of your heretical notions. Remember you are on honor."

The stranger smiled grimly, but made no reply, only to say that he would be happy to render me any service in his power. He had once been a priest, I am certain, for the marks of the tonsure were still upon him; but he was not one now, for he spoke of family ties utterly inconsistent with that sacred office. He was very kind and attentive, and though I felt repelled by his manner, still, as he knew my dear father and Robert, I learned to look upon him almost as an old acquaintance.

One beautiful moonlight evening, as we were walking the deck in company, he said to me in a tone of peculiar meaning:

"You have been away from home for some years, have you not, my young friend?"

"It is six years since I left Scotland," was my reply.

"Shut up as you have been in a convent, you have not probably been fully informed of the great change which has taken place in the land of your birth."

My heart beat quickly, I hardly knew why, as I inquired,

"Of what nature, sir, is the change of which you speak?"

"You may have heard, even in your retirement, of that eminent servant of God George Wishart, who was called to seal his testimony with his blood, having been foully dealt with and murdered by the proud and cruel Cardinal Beaton. The preaching of that blessed martyr was full of power, and the influence thereof spread throughout all Scotland. The great JOHN KNOX, the Paul of this age, was one of the first converts, and now teaches the gospel which he once despised. Your father, Sir Alexander Hope, your brother Robert, and indeed all the family at the Castle, have embraced the doctrines of the Reformation with all their hearts, and most of the nobility have followed their example."

"What is it of which you speak?" I ventured to inquire; "and how do these new doctrines differ from those of the church of Rome?"

"It would be difficult to answer that question in few words, my dear young lady," he replied; "the difference is heaven-wide, and extends to the very foundations of both systems. I can only say that we regard the reformed doctrines as a return to the primitive simplicity of the gospel, as taught by Jesus Christ and his apostles, and from which the Romish church has sadly departed."

"Say no more," I exclaimed; "I am unable to argue with you, and know not how much of sorrow and pain may be before me; but I cannot listen quietly to reflections on the church with which all my hopes of salvation are connected."

The subject was not again brought up between us; and on reaching home, the cordial welcome I received, and my joy in finding myself once more with friends so dear, absorbed my attention until the incident I have related. I said to myself, "I must double my prayers and acts of penance, if by that means I may be the happy instrument of saving those I love from eternal death."

III.

The Family at Hope Castle.

"Though the days that are gone had more canker than blossom,
And even that blossom too tender to last,
Yet had we the power, Oh, where is the bosom
Would thrust from its visions the dreams of the past?"

Oct. 19.

MY friend complains that I have told her nothing about my own family. In truth, when I first came home every thing was new and strange, so that I knew not what to say; and even now, when I have had time to look about me, I am so inexperienced that I hardly dare give my impressions of persons or things, lest they may be wrong. One thing however is certain: my dear parents, brother and sister, are full of kindness and candor towards me, and no one can be with them from day to day without feeling admiration for the spirit which seems to actuate them on all occasions. Never could one imagine a happier or more united household; one in which the law of love is more fully carried out in every relation of life. The servants of the family have grown old in their places, and nothing but death can break the tie that binds them to the family in which all their pride and hopes are centred. But I have promised to give a detailed account of my friends, and I will try to do it as briefly as possible.

My father was a younger son of Sir Robert Hope; and as two older sons stood between him and the succession, he was early taught to feel that he must make his own way in the world, and that on his industry and talent all that was dear to him in the future would depend. He chose the law for his profession, and aided by my grandfather's influence, with his own untiring application, became at an early age Writer to the Signet, and an advocate of wide and increasing popularity. He married the only daughter and co-heiress of Sir Malcolm Dunbar of Lindisfarn, and established himself in Edinburgh, where his three children were born, and where my childhood was spent; and if our house was less splendid than the establishment at the Castle, it was one of the brightest, most cheerful, and well ordered homes imaginable. Every year we all spent several weeks with my grand-parents at this place; and I see them now before me: Sir Robert, with his powdered wig, velvet coat and small-clothes, and gold-headed cane, the ideal of venerable age; and my gentle grandmother, always kind and loving, and yet withal so dignified that her arm-chair seemed a kind of throne, before which we as her subjects paid our homage.

My mother had been greatly admired in her youth, and is even yet one of the most beautiful women I ever saw; but her tastes were simple and domestic, and her heart was with her husband and children, so that she sought no happiness away from them. Never since my remembrance have I heard a word of discord between my parents; never have I known either of them wilfully to disregard the wishes of the other.

Robert is three years older than myself, and attained his majority, amid the rejoicing of the tenantry, a short time previous to my return. I remember him as a studious, high-minded, generous boy; and though I have seen comparatively little of him since coming home, his appearance, together with the general estimation in which he is held, assure me that his character does not belie the promise of his boyhood. His figure is good, and his face full of intelligence, together with a firmness and energy which speak through every feature. When not speaking, his countenance wears an expression of thoughtfulness and almost sadness, that seems to me unsuited to his years. When I rallied him on the subject recently, he replied earnestly:

"You little know, Kathie, how many causes of deep and anxious thought press upon me and all who love our Scotland and her ancient liberties. Our rightful sovereign, far away in a foreign land, a mere girl in the hands of those who hate us; the queen-regent a bigoted foreigner, ignorant of the temper of her subjects, and anxious only to strengthen the power of the house of Guise; and to crown all, the pope and his emissaries striving to regain their lost power in the kingdom. But why should I trouble you with this recital?"

"Rather, why should you not, dear Robert? All that concerns you or my country interests me also, I assure you: but I fear you would be offended if I were to say what I really think on this subject."

"Try me and see," he replied with a smile.

"Pardon me then, my brother, for saying that these new-fangled doctrines seem to me to be at the root of all the evils of which you complain. Strife, sedition, schism, all came in when this fatal door was opened. If you and those who think with you would only come back to the bosom of our holy mother church, all would be well."

"A tender mother she has proved to poor Scotland," he exclained indignantly, "when hanging, burning, and being drawn in quarters were the mildest punishments inflicted on her children for the crime of thinking and reading the Scriptures for themselves. But what can you understand of these things? How can a girl, bred in a foreign convent under the tuition of Jesuit priests, be supposed to know any thing of systems of theology or affairs of state?"

I was hurt at the tone of these remarks, but answered quietly:

"I was bred, as you know, dear brother, where our parents placed me when a child, and do not claim to know much of the subjects you have mentioned. But it cannot require a great deal of intellect or knowledge to resolve to adhere firmly to the faith and the communion which I have been taught to revere as the only true church on earth."

"Pardon me, sweet sister," he said tenderly, "I was severe without cause. The religion I profess ought to have taught me a different lesson."

The entrance of a servant interrupted our conversation, to my great relief; for it is very painful for me to differ from those I love, and this noble brother is very dear to me.

But in what words shall I describe our youngest darling, our golden-haired, violet-eyed Jessie? When I left home, six years ago, I thought her the perfection of lovely, innocent childhood; and on my return I find her the same frank, ingenuous child, with the added sweetness and grace of dawning womanhood But though sportive and unconscious as the pets she loves to collect about her, she has a wisdom and maturity of thought and feeling which make her the trusted friend and companion of our mother;

and even our father talks to her of public affairs, sure of the intelligent sympathy which is so sweet to him.

I tremble for the soul of this beloved sister, whose clinging tenderness makes her every hour dearer to me; and I can only pray the blessed Virgin to protect and bring back to the true fold this wandering lamb. But to return to my narration.

When I was twelve years of age, my godfather and distant relative, Patrick Carr, laird of Ormistoun, who was a childless widower, made me his heiress on two conditions. The first was, that I should be sent at once for education to the convent of St. Denis, in which his deceased wife had been reared, and kept there until I was eighteen. I think that even then the laird of Ormistoun began to fear the influence of those strange doctrines which have now overrun all

Scotland, and wished to save one at least from the fatal influence.

The second condition was different and far more trying. It binds me, on or before reaching the age of twenty-one, to connect myself in marriage with Norman Lyndsay, a nephew of the testator; in default of which, if the failure be on the part of the gentleman, the estate goes to me; if on my part, it reverts to him and his heirs for ever. Of young Lyndsay himself I know nothing. I remember him as a tall, dignified, sedate youth, of whom I felt very much afraid, particularly after any of my youthful escapades, which, I am sorry to say, were very numerous.

Now I hear of him as one of the leaders in the work of reformation, as they call the heresy of Knox and his followers. What will be the end of all this I know not. He seems in no haste to become acquainted with the bride selected for him by his uncle; and on my part I have no wish for an estate so encumbered. Fortunately I am not called on to decide for three years yet to come, as the laird of Ormistoun died some time since; and I shall certainly claim every hour allowed me by the will before making the final decision.

IV.

The New Baronet.

"I hear a voice you cannot hear,
That says I must not stay;
I see a hand you cannot see,
That beckons me away."

DEC. 12, 1558.

SOON after I left home, my uncle Robert, who had been long away from Scotland, and had married disreputably on the continent, was killed instantly in a duel; and as he had no children, uncle Stephen, who, from the cradle, was a hopeless invalid, became heir to the title and estates. The death of her eldest-born broke the heart of my grandmother, who lived but in her children, and she soon sank under the blow. The poor old baronet wandered about sadly and aimlessly, trying to interest himself once more in the plans so suddenly broken in upon; but it was all in vain; he lingered for a few months, and then went to rejoin the wife who, for half a century, had been his constant companion, and whose loss made the earth a desert.

Uncle Stephen was bewildered by the load of responsibility and care thrown upon him; and sending for my father, begged, with tears, that he would have pity upon him, and relieve his anxiety by himself assuming the title and estates. Strong and vigorous as he was, my father could not understand the morbid feeling which prompted this request, and refused it, assuring the poor invalid that the effort would do him good, and that he confidently looked to see him the founder of a family. There may have been some selfish feeling in this, for my father loved his profession and his circle of professional friends, and was wholly unwilling to exchange them even for the grandeur of Hope Castle. But it was soon forced upon him: the poor baronet bore the weight of his unwelcome honors little more than a year, and then was laid to rest beside his father and mother, far more rejoiced to throw off the burden than the new incumbent was to assume it.

It is, however, the universal voice of the tenantry, that never since the days of the good Sir Alexander, who flourished a century ago, has there been a Hope at Hopetown more worthy of the name and appellation than he who now wears the title; indeed I cannot help feeling proud of my dear father when I look at the lands of the castle, with their well-cultivated farms and pleasant cottages, and compare them with the grounds of Languidry, whose owner, though a staunch

Catholic, is too grasping and avaricious to care for the comfort of his dependents.

It is the first wish of my father to interest Robert in all his attempts to improve the condition of the peasantry, so that he may be sure that after his death his plans will be carried out by his successor; indeed, it is beautiful to witness the love and confidence existing between the father and son, and which produces a union so close that they seem like two bodies actuated by but one soul. Did I not know that there can be no salvation out of the pale of the Catholic church, I should feel that lives so filled up with goodness and usefulness must be acceptable to God, and pleasing in his sight; but I would not forget that the enemy of souls takes delight in disguising himself as an angel of light.

I am sure to lose myself in this subject, and will turn from it to introduce the remaining member of our family—the dear aunt Margaret, whom from infancy I have loved so dearly. Dame Margaret Stewart is not in truth my aunt, being only a far-away cousin of my mother; but next to that mother she is loved and venerated by every one in the house, and indeed by all who know her. She is the daughter of the old Lord Ochiltree, who died while she was still young, leaving her with a small fortune at her own disposal, and a person and manners more than usually attractive. A severe disappointment, in the death of one to whom she was betrothed and ardently attached, destroyed her earthly prospects; but instead of retiring from the world into a convent, as so many have done in similar circumstances, this noble woman devoted herself to God by living only for the good of others. Wherever there is sickness or sorrow, aunt Margaret is sure to be found, a ministering spirit at the couch of suffering and the bedside of the dying. For several years she has resided wholly in my father's family, the most devoted and unselfish of friends, always hopeful and cheerful in the darkest hour, and ready to help with hand and brain in every emergency. It would be a dark day for us in which aunt Margaret shall leave Hope Castle, and I trust it may never be while my dear mother lives, for she has been so long accustomed to lean on her as a sister, that I am sure she would feel the loss most keenly.

After what I have said, must I add that, like the rest, this admirable woman is a heretic? Alas, it is even so; and kind as she is to me, I know she looks on me as a blinded, bigoted Papist; while in return I pity her as one who has fallen into the snare of the destroyer. Ah how little I thought, on leaving the peaceful walls of the convent which had sheltered me so long, of the scenes of trial which lay before me. Could I satisfy myself with this world only, I might be merry as the birds of spring, for I am surrounded with love and kindness; but how can I be happy while those dearest to me are in fatal delusion, and exposed to everlasting death? Oh if I could but see Father Francis, and learn from him what is my duty in my present situation, and whether there is any thing which I can do towards bringing back these wandering ones to the true fold. When I look at their pure and useful lives, and contrast them with my own, it seems presumption to think that their souls can be less safe than mine; but since this is the teaching of the holy church, who am I that I should dare to question it?

V.

An Adventure among the Hills.

"Twining memories of old time
With new virtues more sublime."

MAY, 1559.

MY friend seems to think that because I love my family, and speak freely of their virtues, I am therefore in danger of adopting their opinions, and of giving up the faith which is dearer to me than life. For myself, I believe that the danger is not near so great as it would be under other circumstances. If I saw in them less to admire, I might be less careful to guard my own belief from the contagion of example, and so by degrees fall in with those about me, sliding back unconsciously till all was lost. But now I am constantly on my guard;

and though I have not confessed or heard mass since my return, yet in my private devotions I carry out as far as possible, the strictest discipline of the convent rules.

Still, I remember the old fable of the traveller and his cloak. It was not the wind or the storm which tore the garment from his shoulders. They only made him wrap it about him the more closely. It was the sun, pouring his rays so quietly and gently upon him, which compelled him to lay aside the cloak as a useless burden. I trust the moral of this story will not be lost upon me.

Since writing the above, an incident has occurred, which, though trifling in itself, has affected me strangely. It happened on this wise.

My waiting-maid Justine, who came

with me from France, has somehow made acquaintance with a family of Catholics in Perth, and through them she learns much which would otherwise never reach my ears. A few days since, she came to me with a face full of important news, and in reply to my inquiry, told me a sad story of an aged couple who were persecuted by the Protestants for their religion. They had formerly lived, she said, on the Languidry estate; but very recently, their granddaughter, who had always been with them since the death of her father, married a tenant of the Hopetown lands. Very naturally the old people wished to be near her, and came accordingly; but report says they were not permitted to remain, and are now suffering from poverty and sickness among the hills.

I see now that this story carries untruth, or at least exaggeration, on its very face; for where was the grand-daughter while her nearest kindred were dying from destitution? I knew too, that my father was incapable of cruelty or injustice, and I ought to have gone at once to my mother or aunt Margaret with the tale I had heard; but I was just in the humor to make a martyr out of somebody, and to consider this as an affair personal to myself; so I resolved to look into it without assistance from any one but Justine. As my time is entirely at my own command, it was easy to carry out my plan without observation or hinderance.

The walk through the hills was long and tiresome, and more than once I lost my way and was compelled to retrace my steps; but under the guidance of a little shepherd-boy, who was easily induced to go with us, we reached at length the cabin or sheeling, in which the objects of our search had taken refuge.

It was some time after I entered the wretched apartment, before my eyes were able to penetrate the darkness so as to see what was before me. The floor of earth was so uneven that I could hardly make my way across it; the beams that met overhead were blackened with the smoke and dust of centuries; and before a handful of peat which smouldered, instead of burning, sat a couple so withered and old, that they seemed as if waiting for death, who had forgotten them. After several ineffectual attempts, for they were both very deaf, I succeeded in making the old woman understand that I came as a friend; and then her tongue was loosed, and I was completely overpowered by the fierceness of her manner and the rapidity of her utterance.

In vain I tried to explain, to apologize, and promise redress; my words were like straws carried away on the torrent of her wrath, until frightened and disgusted, I wished myself away from the painful scene. Then I saw how foolish I had been. This old woman was evidently an object of pity, wicked and degraded as she was, but in any point of view, it was not a case for the management of a girl. There was nothing that I could do, except to offer them money, and this I knew, among the Scottish peasantry, however poor, would be considered a mortal offence.

So I wisely resolved to do what I should have done before, to place the matter in the hands of my brother on the first opportunity; and deeply humbled, left the cabin, followed by muttered execrations instead of the blessings I had anticipated. In my confusion and trouble, I took a path in the opposite direction from that in which my little guide had led me; and before finding out my error, had travelled a long way from Hope Castle instead of towards it. The glens grew narrower, the ravines wilder, the hills in a thousand fantastic shapes seemed closing in about me, and just in front, a mountain torrent fell with loud noise into a dark and deep abyss. In a word, I was lost—completely and hopelessly lost—for of these hills and forests I knew nothing; and as the sun was obscured by clouds, I had no idea of the direction in which my distant home lay. Justine was helpless as a child, and added to my perplexity by her tears and lamentations, declaring that we were justly punished for having consented to live with heretics, and that if the Virgin would only hear and deliver us, she would henceforth shut her eyes and ears against all but members of the true church. I too, felt that the punishment was just, but it was myself I blamed, not the beloved ones whose pure and useful lives shamed the indolence of mine.

In this emergency, when we feared to take another step, lest it might lead us further astray, imagine my delight on seeing a gentleman on horseback emerging from a side path just behind us. Without a moment's hesitation, I approached him, and stating our case, begged for help and guidance. We must have looked like two forlorn damsels, for the stranger could scarcely repress a smile as he answered with genuine kindness, that he would be happy to render us any assistance in his power. We were obliged to turn about, but not to go over again the wearisome road we had travelled, as our guide led us by a shorter cut through the woods, beguiling the way by remarks so full of spirit and interest, that I forgot my fatigue, and thought only of the pleasure I was enjoying.

You know me to be a creature of impulse, and at that moment the impulse was strong upon me to tell my new acquaintance the errand which had led me into this wild region, and the reports I had heard; but though my father was not named, the stranger evidently understood the case, and exclaimed as I ended:

"Could you then, for an instant, believe such an idle story as this, and about a man like Sir Alexander Hope, when there is not a child on his estate who does not know that in him the poorest and most degraded always find a friend? You must indeed have been ignorant of the character of that excellent man."

"But it was on account of their religion, you know," I replied, greatly ashamed to find a stranger taking a view of the subject so much more just to my dear father than that of his own daughter.

"As if their religion could make any difference," he said, almost indignantly; "unless it were to render him more lenient on that account. Depend upon it, lady, your kindness has been abused. The whole thing bears falsehood on its face, and no one who knows Sir Alexander as I do, could believe it for a moment."

In spite of deserved mortification, my heart warmed towards the stranger who thus defended my father, and I exclaimed involuntarily:

"Oh, why should such a man as you have described, so generous, so noble, fall a victim to the snare of the enemy of souls?"

"Ask rather," replied my companion, "how such a man could avoid seeing and welcoming the light, when once its rays have fallen upon him. It is not the weak and ignorant who have become followers of Knox and Wishart in our land. The very flower of the nobility, and of the priesthood too, have embraced the doctrines of the reformation; and in spite of the court, aye, and of the devil, their number will increase, until the whole realm is brought back to God."

Why was it that I found it so difficult to answer this stranger? Not surely because his words made any impression upon me, for my whole soul was in arms against them; but there was something so attractive in his earnest face, so much dignity and nobleness in his tone and manner, that I was spellbound in his presence, and found it impossible to collect my thoughts. He must have seen and pitied my embarrassment, for he dropped the subject, and conversed on indifferent matters till we came out on the banks of the Tay, a short distance below the Castle.

As he was turning his horse's head to depart, I ventured to say,

"Since you are acquainted with my father, sir, shall we not soon see you at the Castle, that I may thank you properly for the great service you have rendered me?"

Without replying to my question, he said, as if to himself,

"I was not mistaken, then; this is the long absent daughter, the Kathie of whom I have heard so much. Many thanks, lady, for your kind invitation; doubt not we shall soon meet again."

For various reasons, nothing was said by me on reaching home of this meeting with a stranger among the hills. But it was not the less in my thoughts, and I wearied myself in trying to conjecture who my unknown guide might be. Once or twice the truth flashed over my mind, but I refused to entertain it for a moment. It was impossible that Norman Lyndsay, of whom I had always thought as a pale, studious youth, could have become a bronzed and bearded man like this; and then, surely he would have made himself known to me. Altogether, my thoughts were full of the affair, and would not turn in any other direction.

VI.

Visitors at the Castle.

"There is an electric chord uniting hearts, however distant, that beat in unison, which, when once touched by the master-hand, will continue to vibrate, making heavenly harmonies to all eternity."

JUNE.

A FEW days after the incident related in my last, as we were all—that is, my parents, Robert, Jessie, and myself—seated in my mother's pleasant dressing-room, visitors were announced, and I heard the names of Melville and Lyndsay from the servant. When they entered the room, I saw in the younger of the two, who was introduced to me as Norman Lyndsay, the stranger who had appeared so opportunely in the wood, and my face flushed painfully as I rose to receive him. He smiled as he took my offered hand, but made no allusion to our previous meeting; and having kindly welcomed me home, passed on to my mother and sister, by whom he was received with a warmth of affection which surprised me, as I had heard his name so seldom mentioned since coming home.

Mr. Lyndsay is above the common height, finely formed, and full of quiet dignity in manner and movement. He is dark, and his face in repose is rather stern in expression; but when speaking, it lights up wonderfully, and one reads in it so much truth and goodness, that it wins upon the confidence far more than mere physical beauty.

He conversed for some time in a low tone with my father on affairs of state; then turning to my mother, said pleasantly:

"I am very glad, my dear madam, to be the first to bring you what I know will be good news. Last week, your brother, Sir James Dunbar, and his children, returned to Lindisfarn."

"It is, then, true," replied my mother. "This is good news indeed. We heard they were coming, but knew not whether to believe it, they had become so attached to Germany."

"Are both Max and Veronica with their father?" inquired Robert eagerly.

"So I have been told, though I saw only Max on my recent call at Lindisfarn. I regret to say he seems to care more for boating and racing, for his dogs and horses, than for the great interests which divide the nation; though Sir James, who naturally looks on the bright side, assures me that Max is Protestant at heart, and will be ready to act when the occasion shall present itself."

"God grant it may be so," exclaimed my mother fervently. "He would be unworthy the name he bears if he could care more for his own selfish pleasures than for the interests of the suffering church of God. My brother was ever an ardent lover of freedom, and the intercourse he has for years enjoyed with the leading reformers of Germany and Holland, has deepened his early convictions into fixed principles of action."

"The time for action may come sooner than he thinks," said Master Melville, who till now had not spoken; "the cup of indignation is nearly full. This foreign domination over the consciences of freeborn men has become intolerable; and priest-ridden as she was so long, Scotland has yet many sons who will dare as much for religious freedom as Wallace and Bruce could dare for civil liberty."

"Our brethren in the Netherlands," remarked Norman Lyndsay, "who are so bravely maintaining their liberties against the crafty and cruel Philip, look with anxious interest on the faithful in Scotland for the sympathy and assistance so needful and precious to them. William of Orange, one of the noblest princes ever placed by God over a free people, is sore bestead, and unless he have speedy help from God or man, may be compelled to yield to his enemies. But for the necessity of attending to my worldly affairs, I would ere this have been fighting by his side; and I trust ere long to be there, unless, as may well prove, the swords of all her children are needed in our own distracted country. The queen-regent is now lying dangerously sick in the castle of Edinburgh, and the priests who have her confidence talk loudly of the speedy return of her daughter, Queen Mary."

"Alas," exclaimed my father, "I fear

the change bodes us little good. Trained, as our young queen has been, in the most profligate court of Europe, and wholly under the influence of her uncles of the house of Guise, the implacable enemies of the true faith, what can be expected from her coming but new sources of trouble and dispute?"

"Those who have known her royal highness in France," replied Norman Lyndsay, "speak of her as inclined towards lenity and moderation, though she is wholly devoted to the church of Rome. Still, we know that the Catholic priesthood always have the ear of the sovereign, and that her own private feelings will not be suffered to control her public acts. But I fear," he added, turning to me with that winning manner which had already impressed me so favorably, "that our conversation can have but little interest for your daughter, though I am sure that, as a true Hope, she carries a leal Scottish heart within her bosom."

Although I could not fully understand all that had been said, enough of it was intelligible to show me that I stood alone among the enemies of my faith, and I answered impetuously,

"Every thing that concerns those I love interests me; but it can hardly be expected that, educated as I have been in France and in the bosom of the Catholic church, I should share in the hatred of both, which all around me seem to feel."

My father and Master Melville were in the embrasure of a distant window, conversing earnestly at the moment, so that my rude speech was unheard by them; but my mother instantly replied:

"My child, you forget yourself in uttering a sentiment like that. I am certain it was never prompted by the heart of my Kathie."

These words touched me deeply; but the kind eyes that had always beamed on me with love from my earliest remembrance, now dimmed with tears for my sake, penetrated my very soul, and throwing myself on a low stool at her feet, I exclaimed,

"Forgive me, dear mother. I know I am rash and wayward; but my heart is very sad, and I hardly know what I say. It is so hard to feel that I am all alone among my kindred in the belief which was taught me from childhood, and which I at least have never seen any reason for abandoning. I cannot change my faith as I would a garment which chanced to be displeasing in your sight."

"My dear child," she answered, embracing me tenderly, "you have never been requested to do so. We all love you fondly, and desire only your best interests for both worlds. Trust in us, my love; and let us only have patience with each other, and all will yet be well."

After a little more desultory conversation our visitors departed, and since they left us nothing of interest has occurred, only that all my friends seem, if possible, kinder and more desirous of studying my happiness than ever before.

The sun is shining warmly and brightly on the traveller: will it rob him of his cloak? I still think not; but time only can determine.

VII.

Days of Darkness.

"The morning cometh, and also the night.'

MARCH, 1560.

IT is long since I communed with my faithful journal, but I have had much to occupy my thoughts of late; and our domestic quiet has been broken in upon by the most strange and unexpected events. First came the return of Sir James Dunbar, my mother's half-brother, from Germany, with his children, Max and Veronica. But I am not going to tell you about them here, for Veronica, my lovely cousin, deserves a whole page to herself, and some time I will try to describe her as she seems to me, but not now.

Then my father and Sir James Melville were sent by the reformers here on a special mission to England, after the death of the queen-regent; and Oh, what a time of anxiety and terror followed their departure. That it was a journey full of danger we all knew, for the pride and jealousy of Queen Elizabeth rendered her equally capricious to friends and enemies, and few there were who would have had the courage to brave the perils that awaited them in London. But with all his quietness and reserve, my father is afraid of nothing but sin; and Sir James is equally incapable of fear; so they freely accepted the trust offered them, and some months since left us for England.

For many weeks little was heard of them, save that obstacles of various kinds were placed in their way by the advisors of the queen. At length Norman Lyndsay and Master Andrew Melville, a preacher of the reformed faith, and a close friend of my father, came to the Castle and inquired for my mother. It was long since we had seen Master Lyndsay, and the moment I looked in his face I knew he had heavy tidings to impart; and so it proved. My father and uncle were both close prisoners, confined in different apartments of the Tower, on pretence of treasonable designs, but in reality because the queen had heard that her rival Mary was soon to embark for Scotland. What would be the result it was impossible to foretell, but from what we knew of the Tudor blood, there was reason to fear that the prisoners would be freed only by a summons to the scaffold.

What dreadful news was this to fall suddenly on the ears of wife and children, to whom those threatened lives were dearer than their own! For the first time in my life I was tempted to murmur at the severity of the Romish church, supposing that, like her sister, Elizabeth was a member of that communion; but when informed that she was a Protestant, my indignation knew no bounds. I called upon all the saints to help us, and to punish the cruel queen for her injustice and intolerance. Was this a wrong feeling? If so, may the blessed Virgin forgive me, for indeed I could not help it.

Never shall I forget the kindness of Master Lyndsay in this time of sorrow The suffering he saw, but could not alleviate, opened his heart, and showed it to us as years of ordinary intercourse would not have done. How tenderly he tried to prepare us for the sad intelligence! How truly and deeply he sympathized in the anguish he had not the power to avert!

True heart! grand and noble soul! Our differing creeds may separate us for ever; but I have at least learned to do justice to the purity and excellence of his character, and to feel that, heretic as he is, all my ideas of manly worth and true nobleness are more than realized in him. And yet, though his eye seems ever upon me, and his kind attentions are unceasing, he seldom speaks to me, and is far more at his ease with Jessie than with me. Perhaps he despises me for what he may call my bigoted adherence to the faith he has forsaken, and wishes me to understand his feelings.

But no, let me not do him this injustice. A heart like his cannot despise any of God's creatures; and there are times when I am almost certain that he feels an interest in my happiness. The truth is, I do not know what I do really think or feel in relation to this most singular, inexplicable man; so generous and kind, yet so cold and reticent; so pure in heart and life, yet so hopelessly perverted from the truth; so forgetful of self, and yet so immovable in his prejudices and opinions: all these things make his character a riddle which it is impossible to read. But let it pass. What can there be in common between us, separated as we are by a gulf across which no bridge can ever safely be thrown?

Master Andrew Melville, his associate and friend, is a thin, wiry man, whose restless and energetic soul seems to have worn away the frail body to the extreme of attenuation. But his eye is full of intellect and life; and when he proposed starting at once for England to see what could be done for our dear friends there, I could have knelt before him with tears of gratitude and admiration. But my mother, while she thanked him for the kindness of the proposal, saw at once how worse than useless it would be, since it would only add another to the number of the victims. So we could only hope and wait; and Robert went constantly between Hope Castle and Lindisfarn trying to comfort Max and Veronica, and then coming home to weep and pray with us. I say with *us*, for I confess that in this time of sorrow there is something very soothing to me in the petitions poured forth by my friends to Jesus the Saviour of sinners, and not all the litanies I could repeat to the blessed Virgin and the saints could give me equal comfort. Of course the fault was in myself, and not in the church of which I am a faithful though unworthy member, and which must have rich consolations for those of her children who are wise enough to appreciate them.

After a long, long period of suspense,

during which we knew not whether to think of our beloved friends as among the living or the dead, our hearts were gladdened by good tidings, and in a few more days we had the unspeakable happiness of seeing them once more. The queen, who seems to me to enjoy the agony she inflicts on human hearts, kept her noble captives long in doubt as to what their fate was to be; and then released as she had imprisoned them, without deigning to make any explanation or apology. Were Scotland what it once was, in the days of yore, this imperious Elizabeth would be compelled to account for her unworthy treatment of Scottish noblemen; but situated as we are, without a head, divided by innumerable feuds, and weakened by the fatal consequences of Flodden Field, we can only bear in sullen silence the indignities heaped upon us by our misproud neighbor.

Notwithstanding his long and painful detention, my dear father came home satisfied and happy in the success of his mission, which, thanks to the influence of the queen's ministers, was carried through in spite of her coldness and double-dealing. I do not quite understand the business which took my father to England, but it was something relating to universal toleration; a subject which lies very near his heart.

One thing in relation to this subject I cannot but observe: when the Catholics are in power they seem to think it not only right but necessary to propagate their religion by fire and sword; but when they are on the losing side no party cry more loudly for toleration than they. If it is acceptable to God for men to force their own belief upon their fellow-creatures under any circumstances, it must surely be the duty of

Protestants no less than Catholics. But I will not suffer myself to pursue this train of thought, of which, after all, I understand nothing. My father stayed with us for a few days only, and then went to Edinburgh to meet the lords of the privy council, where he has been ever since.

VIII.

The Apostle of Scotland.

"John Knox was a man of fearless heart and fluent eloquence; violent perhaps, and sometimes coarse, but the better fitted to obtain influence in a coarse and turbulent age. He was capable at once of reasoning with the wiser nobility, and of inspiring with his own spirit and zeal the fierce populace; and his deficiency in the softer graces only made him the more fit to play the distinguished part to which he was called."

JUNE 24.

I HAD been out walking recently, when on my return I found two strangers in my mother's room, one of whom was John Knox, the arch-heretic, and the other our old friend, Master Andrew Melville. The great reformer is a tall, slender man, with a flowing beard falling to his breast, and a countenance which, though very grave, is marked with sincerity and kindness. He received me with courtesy, as the child of his friend, and laying his hand on my head, said solemnly, "The Lord bless thee, my daughter; the Lord lift up the light of his countenance upon thee, and make thee a blessing to thy father's house, and to the church of the living God."

Was it wrong that my heart thrilled when I heard these words, and that my lips framed an involuntary amen? If I were sure it was wrong, I would ask Father Francis to impose upon me any penance he sees fit, for I freely acknowledge the fact, and confess also that I cannot help listening with pleasure to his conversation. He loves Scotland and liberty so dearly, that my Scottish heart leaps up at the tones of his rich, deep voice, as at the sound of a trumpet.

Then too he speaks so sweetly of the love of God in sending his Son to die upon the cross for poor ruined man;

of our lost condition by nature, and the hopes and joys of the believer in Christ, that ere I am aware I often find tears dropping fast upon my embroidery-frame. Why is it, that this name of Jesus, when it finds an entrance into the human heart, awakens an echo there which sounds even to its inmost depths? I cannot help loving to repeat it softly to myself when alone; and though, from fear of committing sin, I have doubled my prayers to the blessed Virgin and my patron saint, yet they fall coldly on my ear in comparison with that mysterious name. But I must dismiss these thoughts, which trouble my mind without doing any good, and go on with my narration.

Master Knox had not been long with us when I learned from my mother that he was a widower, his English wife having died some time since, and that his errand here is to carry away, if he can so persuade her, Dame Margaret Stewart—our own dear aunt Margaret. This most unwelcome news brought back all my former dislike to the heretic preacher, and without thought I exclaimed,

"What next? Is it not enough that by his arts he has drawn all I love best away from the truth, but he must rob us of aunt Margaret also? Would to God we had never seen his face."

My mother's look was troubled, but her voice gentle as ever as she replied,

"My dear child, I hoped that one so truly excellent as Master Knox might ere this have found his way to your heart. He is the friend of your parents, and as far as mortal man may be so, their guide and counsellor; and I am sure the kind heart of my Kathie will not reject him for a mere prejudice."

"Do you call it prejudice," I replied.

"to hold fast to the truths I have always been taught to believe, and to shudder when I see all that I love turning away from them? I look on this man as a perverter of souls, and feel that it is almost a deadly sin to regard him with approbation or even patience."

A deep sigh was my mother's only answer, but I saw her lips move as if in prayer; while my sister, throwing her arms about my neck, exclaimed,

"Darling Kathie, if we cannot agree perfectly in our belief, we can certainly be united in heart while we both worship the same Saviour, and love the same friends and kindred on earth. We pray constantly for you, and I doubt not that you also pray for us; why should we not then be patient and forbearing towards each other until God in his mercy shall cause us all to walk together in the same narrow path of life?"

"If that time ever comes," I said, "it must be by your returning to the true faith; for never will I relinquish all hope of salvation by adopting your belief."

"If we truly seek His face," she answered with a smile, "God will lead us into the truth. I believe this with all my heart, and am willing to wait his time for its fulfilment."

I could not say any thing unkind to so sweet a pleader, and as my head ached violently, I retired to my own room, more depressed and discouraged than I had ever yet been. It is hard to resist the silent pleading of my own treacherous heart, the example of my friends, and the influence of all around me; but I have no thought of yielding, and from what I have heard recently have some hope that brighter days are at hand. Master Knox, who has just come from

Edinburgh, told my father that news had arrived of the death of king Francis, adding with seeming joy that "his glory had perished, and the pride of his stubborn heart vanished into smoke." Our own queen Mary is now a widow, and will undoubtedly return to her native land, and ascend the throne so long vacant. Young, beautiful, and all-perfect as she is, who can resist her fascination? She is a true daughter of our holy church, and will therefore favor the Catholic religion, while she is too mild and good to allow of cruelty towards those who differ from her in faith.

I have seen this lovely woman several times in France, and she looked almost like an angel, smiling and bowing to all around her with a grace peculiarly her own. I cannot help hoping that when she is settled at Holyrood I may have some place near her, for it must be happiness to be in her presence daily, to hear those sweet tones, and look upon that bright face so full of feeling; and then too I could enjoy the exercise of my own religion, as I never have done since leaving France. But these are daydreams, and I will say no more about them.

IX.

Broken Cisterns.

"Oh, thou who driest the mourner's tear,
How dark this world would be,
If, when deceived and wounded here,
We could not fly to thee."

AUGUST 13.

THE ceremony is over, and aunt Margaret Stewart is now dame Margaret Knox, and has left us for Edinburgh, with her newly-made bridegroom. She will prove a treasure to her husband, for her nature is all love and self-devotion, while at the same time she is firmness itself in resisting what she believes to be wrong, or in maintaining the right. We shall miss her sorely, but Master Knox seems so happy in her society, and so full of gratitude to God for the treasure he has given him, that I cannot find it in my heart to grudge him the gift. Just before leaving the Castle, he held a long conversation with me, nearly as follows:

I had been in the fields gathering flowers, and came very near stepping on a poisonous serpent which lay coiled up under a stone. Fortunately I saw the danger just in time to avoid it. I was relating the circumstance to Jessie, and made use of the expression, "Thanks to the Madonna, I escaped without harm."

"Ah, child," exclaimed a voice from the window-seat, in which unseen by me, Master Knox sat reading; "do not thank a creature like yourself for such a preservation. Rather thank God who saved you, than a woman who, though favored and blessed above all other women, had, while on earth, no power even to protect herself."

"That may be your belief," I answered quickly, and I fear without due respect; "but it is not mine, and I trust never will be."

He laid by his book, and motioning me to a seat at his side, said in his gentlest tone,

"My daughter, I have seen very little of you, but that little has led me to feel that you have a kind and affectionate heart—one that would not willingly give pain to any human being. Why is it then, that you turn away so resolutely from those dearest to you, that you refuse to examine the grounds of their belief, or to admit the possibility of a mistake in your own?"

How could I, a weak and ignorant young girl, meet this man, unmatched throughout the kingdom for wisdom and eloquence? But I was fairly driven to bay, and in such a case the most timid animal acquires courage.

"It is indeed a bitter thing," I replied, "to find myself alone among my kindred; but the faith I profess, is unfortunately not like a garment, to be put on or off at pleasure, or altered and trimmed to suit the fashion of the times. I cannot hold an argument with you, but I can suffer, and I trust, if need were, even die for my belief."

"I doubt it not, my young friend," he answered calmly; "but believe me, sincerity and earnestness in our faith are no proof of its correctness. If you are building your hopes for heaven on any thing besides the finished work and righteousness of the Redeemer, you will surely find all other foundation to be but hay, wood, and stubble, in the day that shall try men's work so as by fire. There is no other name but the name of Jesus given among men by which we can be saved; and the saints on whom you call not only have no power to help you, but must themselves look for salvation only through his blood."

"Our holy church believes in the Saviour," I said, struggling against the impression his words made upon me; "in what respect does your new faith differ from that taught by her?"

"Gladly will I tell you, child, if you have the patience to listen. Your church differs from ours in having substituted a thousand things of man's device for the simple truths of the gospel, as taught by Jesus Christ and his apostles. We are told in the Bible that the way of salvation as revealed there is so plain that the wayfaring man, though a fool, need not err therein; but your priests declare that the unlearned can only find it through their aid, and forbid the laity to read the word of God, lest they should wrest it to their own destruction.

Like the Pharisees of old, they load men's consciences with burdens of fasts, penances, mortifications, and such like, grievous to be borne, though they know that the great Teacher says, 'My yoke is easy, and my burden is light.' They will not allow you in prayer to come directly to Him who is the only Mediator between God and man, but teach you to address innumerable saints, who when here in the flesh were sinners like others, and who were saved, if they are now in heaven, only by faith in Christ. God says through the apostle Paul, 'Now the just shall live by faith.' But the priests say they are to live by unmeaning prayers repeated in a dead language, of which the common people know nothing; by rites and ceremonies, by liberal contributions to the priesthood, and by mortifying and ill-treating the body; thus taking for truth the traditions of men. The Protestants have thrown off this intolerable load, and gone back to the simplicity of the primitive church, taking God at his word, and trusting him alone for salvation, as he is freely offered in the gospel. They would place the holy Scriptures in the hands of all, believing them able to make men wise unto salvation, if they are received in the heart and carried out in the life. Do you not see from this brief statement, how widely the two systems differ, and can you doubt on which side the truth is to be found?"

Staggered, but not convinced, I replied,

"Unskilled as I am in theology, you are not to conclude that because I cannot answer you I have therefore the worst of the argument. Your reasoning has been answered many times by the fathers of the church, but my duty as a private member and a woman, is to believe and not to argue."

"Your duty is to examine for yourself," he said, with some severity of manner; "and you will be held strictly to it. God has committed your soul to your own keeping, and no other one can answer for it, whatever your priests may tell you."

His words fell heavily upon my heart, and something within seemed to tell me, "they are truth;" but I was distressed and frightened at the thought, and hastily rising, I assumed a lightness I was far from feeling, as I said,

"I shall have to do penance for the sin of listening to this long homily from a heretic, and must now run away in self-defence."

When I reached my own apartment, however, I shed tears of vexation and shame over the flippancy of my behavior, and the want of right feeling which I had exhibited.

The next day the good man, for such, however mistaken, I do believe him to be, left us; and in his eye, as he bade me farewell, there was a world of tender and solemn meaning, which pricked me to the heart, and could not be shaken off even after his departure.

But my thoughts were soon diverted from this subject by an event which has shaken the kingdom to its foundations. The Lord James Gowrie, a nobleman who was the friend and pupil of Cardinal Beaton, and who, since the murder of the primate, has been at the head of the Catholic interest in Scotland, was found recently, dead in his room in the palace of St. Andrew's. From the appearance of the body and the circumstances attending it, he must have died by violence, and universal report points to Norman Lyndsay as the instigator of the deed. My heart refuses to believe the dreadful story, even while my pen records it. It cannot be that a man like him, so high-minded, generous and pure, should sanction the midnight murder even of his worst enemy, much less of a nobleman so high in church and state as Lord Gowrie. My father and all the rest evidently shun conversation with me, though they are thoughtful, and even sad, and messengers are coming and going to and fro continually.

Last night, after I had retired to my own room, I heard the sounds of an arrival at the Castle, and Justine says that long after midnight there were voices in earnest conversation in the library. What can it mean? I am surrounded with mystery, and cannot see my way through the labyrinth.

After dinner, as I entered my mother's room, she called me to her, and said kindly,

"My love, I think it right to tell you that Norman Lyndsay was here last night, and that common fame charges him with the murder of Lord Gowrie."

My face must have been deadly pale, as I exclaimed,

"But of course, my mother, this charge is utterly, basely false. Norman Lyndsay could not be guilty of such a crime. Tell me you do n't believe it for a moment, or I think I shall go mad."

"How, my dear child, shall I make you understand what I do believe on this subject, without doing myself or another injustice? I regard Master Lyndsay as one of the noblest of men, and am sure if he sanctioned this deed, that there are reasons which fully justify him in his own eyes, for he is one who would feel dishonor like a wound. But his ideas of duty and patriotism are, I fear, more Roman than Christian, and the deceased nobleman has been the bitterest enemy of the Reformation in Scotland. Added to this, a feud has long existed between the family of Buchan, to which Lyndsay belongs, and that of Lord James Gowrie; and in our country, you know, the unholy system of revenge has taken root even in the noblest minds. Our friend, though he does not acknowledge the deed, will not deny it, but maintains an inflexible silence when questioned concerning it."

"All this does not prove his guilt," I exclaimed with vehemence; "and never will I believe it till his own lips have confessed him a murderer. The very thought is monstrous, and I for one refuse to harbor it."

But while I spoke so confidently, my heart was torn with conflicting emotions, and the very earth seemed sliding from beneath my feet. How I gained my room I know not, but once there I threw myself on the couch, and burying my head in the pillows, wept the bitterest tears of my whole life. Now when all was over between us, I learned how much the seemingly noble qualities of this man had gained upon me, and felt that, young as I was, the brightness and sparkle of life had gone from me for ever. But I think that even then, the sorrow I felt was less for the destruction of my own hopes, than for the loss of my faith in human nature. If such a man had sinned so miserably, who could henceforth be found worthy of trust? If high birth, rich gifts of mind and person, and all noble and engaging qualities, have failed to secure their possessor from a fall like this, what can be expected of those less splendidly endowed?

They were long and bitter hours spent by me in these reflections, but they have done me good, for they have taught me the necessity of a more strict adherence to the faith in which I have been educated. Nothing but heresy could so have perverted that grand soul, as to make it possible for him to commit a crime like this.

My mother and sister are all love and kindness to me in this time of trial. Indeed, my friend, the religion of these beloved ones is a very attractive thing. It is not so much a system as a habit; not a dry theory, but a continual and daily act of charity and self-abnegation. Their piety is so deep and pervading, so simple and unaffected, that I feel in their presence as if breathing a pure atmosphere, in which envy, evil-speaking, and strife, insensibly melt away and vanish.

My cousin Veronica too, has been here often, and her presence is inexpressibly soothing to me. I am not in general attracted to strangers, but on my first meeting with this dear cousin, I was drawn to her by a tie that has grown stronger with each interview.

The Lyndsays, together with Master Knox, have been maintaining the Castle of St. Andrew's against a large body of men, Catholics and foreigners, who have besieged it. Norman Lyndsay is hereditary castellan of this almost impregnable fortress, and while there, can bid defiance to his enemies. But stone walls and deep moats are no protection against the wrath of God, and sooner or later it will severely fall upon the guilty. Deep down in my heart, carefully hidden from sight, is a conviction that this man is innocent of the crime alleged against him; but as I can give no reason for the feeling, it will probably never be uttered by me.

The court party are full of indignation and bitterness, and warrants have been issued for the apprehension of the suspected persons. Robert says as soon as the popular feeling has in a measure subsided, Norman Lyndsay will undoubtedly carry out his plan of joining the army of the prince of Orange, and leave Scotland, perhaps for ever. I know this is best, but it is hard to feel it, for when did the heart ever take counsel of expediency?

X.

A Visit to Edinburgh.

"I came to the home of my youth, and I said, 'The friends of my youth, where are they?' And echo answered, 'Where are they?'"

Nov. 18.

SINCE writing last I have visited Aberdeen, Glasgow, and above all Edinburgh, the early home which for years has so haunted my sleeping and waking dreams. Robert, Max, and Veronica were with me, and in their company I have gone over all the scenes of my childish joys and sorrows; but alas, they are no longer the same. A certain sadness seems to brood over them all, and when I ask, Where are the joys which hope promised in those coming years to which I looked so eagerly? an echo in my own soul answers, "Where?" As we wandered over the rooms in the dear old house, now tenanted by strangers, which were pictured so faithfully by memory, they looked dark and gloomy, even when lighted up by Veronica's sweet face and bright smile; and "mother's room," that blessed retreat of childhood, was now a playroom for rude boys, and full of all the varieties of rubbish they are sure to collect about them. This desecration cost me so many tears, that my companions drew me away from the house, pitying the weakness with which they were unable to sympathize.

We went next to Calton Hill and St. Leonard's crags, the favorite resorts of our childhood, where with Jenny, our faithful nurse and friend, we were permitted to wander at will, on those sweet summer afternoons when all nature seems to smile, and the mere consciousness of existence fills the heart with gladness even to overflowing. But the charm was all gone, and even the splendid views from Arthur's Seat and the castle, which once would have moved me to tears, now failed to awaken any enthusiasm, for the pall of desolation is spread over them all.

Veronica insists upon it that the change is in my own feelings, and that to her every thing looks enchanting as the garden of Eden when the eyes of the first pair were opened upon the newly created world. She may be right; but is it possible that one's own feelings can thus rob the face of nature of all its brightness and beauty? If so, there is a more close and subtle connection between all the things God has made, animate and inanimate, than I have supposed possible.

But to return. We all went through the abbey of Holyrood, once the habitation of monks, but now a kingly palace, and were interested in the preparations making for the reception of our beautiful queen, whom may the holy Virgin protect and bring safely back to us; for surely poor Scotland, worn and scarred by intestine broils and feuds, has sore need of her rightful sovereign.

Veronica and I were introduced without formality to the Lord James Stewart, natural brother of the queen, who since the death of the regent presides over the privy council and in the halls of Holyrood. He was formerly prior of St. Andrew's, but has embraced the doctrines of the Reformation, outwardly at least, and of course no longer holds that office. We were received very graciously, and a wish expressed by his lordship that when the household of the queen was appointed we should both accept the situation of maids of honor near her person. The proposal was politely but firmly declined by Veronica; but I made little reply, as without the permission of my parents it would be impossible for me to accept it, however grateful to my feelings such a position might be. The Catholics everywhere are looking up, for they know that when the queen arrives her influence will be exerted in their behalf, and under such a sovereign court influence must be very powerful, even though silently exerted.

We have seen Master Knox once, but dear aunt Margaret was not with him. The family with whom we board are ardent friends of the preacher, who, since leaving St. Andrew's, spends most of his time in the city. It is not possible, even in one's own mind, on looking into the face of this good and great man, to think of him with any feeling but confidence and respect. He denounces the murder of Lord Gowrie in strong terms, though he says it is a striking instance of the retributive justice of God, working by means of guilty instruments.

To my great joy, Robert inquired of him concerning Norman Lyndsay, of whom I longed to hear, though, had my life depended upon it, I could not have pronounced the name.

"He is still at the castle," was the reply, "cool, calm, and courageous as ever, and apparently as unconscious of wrong in that matter as if he had never till now heard of it. I have little doubt that this noble young man is for some reason bearing a stigma which does not belong to him, for I have good reason to know that his conscience is tender, and could not lightly endure the stain of such a crime. He will suffer in silence, believing that in his own time God will vindicate his innocence, and feeling that meantime he will 'make the wrath of man to praise him,' by overruling it to the advancement of his own cause."

"But, my good sir," inquired Robert with a smile, "does not this idea savor a little of the jesuitical doctrine that 'the end sanctifies the means,' and that we may do evil that good may come?"

"Remember, my young friend," he replied gravely, "that the words are not mine, but His who cannot lie; and moreover that in applying them in this case, I am giving you not my own opinion, but that of another, who truly believes that the death of the lord of Gowrie was a judicial act, deserved by a thousand crimes against God and man. You know well that we have no sympathy with that most infamous dogma, and that we believe ourselves forbidden by God to take into our own hands the vengeance which belongeth only unto him."

"Pardon me, dear sir," said my brother; "I do indeed know that your teaching has always been of a kind directly opposite, and I have never for a moment believed that you could sanction that bloody deed; but will my brave friend long bear to be shut up in that stronghold, like a wild beast in a cage, when everywhere abroad there is so much need of the stout arm and the heavy blow in defence of the good cause? The unwonted restraint must chafe his spirit sorely."

"He will remain to defend the castle while his help is needed; then he intends going to the continent, probably to the Netherlands, to fight under the standard of William of Orange against the cruel and unrelenting Spaniards. I am sure," he added, turning to me, "that I run no risk in speaking of this intention here, where all are friends to

Master Lyndsay, though we are not all believers in the same faith."

I was irritated by the implied doubt, and replied hastily,

"You need have no fear of me. I have been taught to regard Lord James Gowrie as a leader in the church, and lament his cruel death; but though from my heart I detest his murderers, whoever they may be, I am a Hope, and have in me nothing of the stuff out of which informers are made."

"Well said, my cousin," whispered Veronica; "I am glad to see one little flash of your old spirit once more. I was afraid you were becoming a very insipid Hope, you have been so quiet and passive of late; but this inspires me with fresh courage."

"I did not doubt our young friend," Master Knox said; "but knowing the stringency of the rules of the Catholic church in this respect, feared there might be some conflict between her kind heart and honorable feelings, and her sense of duty to that church."

I did not reply, for the momentary excitement was over, and my heart had sunk down again heavy as lead within my bosom. Oh why do not the Holy Mother and the saints hear the invocations I address to them night and day, and restore peace to my soul? Others have suffered far more severely than I, yet they are calm and happy, while I am tempest-tossed and without comfort. Whence is this difference? Veronica, of whom I once asked this question, says it is because I do not go to the right Source for help and strength; but can a young girl like her know better than all the fathers of our church? She says that all who carry their sorrows to Jesus, the Saviour and Friend of sinners, either find them removed, or strength given to bear them, and a strange joy and peace filling their souls. If this is so, why have I never heard of it from my spiritual teachers and guides? I seem to be wandering in a maze, from which there is no visible way of escape. Pity me, holy Saint Catharine, and remember me in your daily orisons, for I need your prayers.

XI.

My Cousin Veronica.

'In her utmost lightness there is truth, and often she speaks lightly,
And she has a grace in being gay, which even mourners approve;
For the root of some grave earnest thought is understruck so rightly,
As to justify the foliage and the waving flowers above."

April, 1561.

VERONICA came with us to Hope Castle, and remained here more than a month, filling every part of the old building with a light and gladness it never knew before. When I saw her flitting through the dark galleries and sombre apartments of the ancient keep, it seemed as though a sunbeam entered with her, brightening every thing on which it fell. How shall I fitly describe her, this bright, loving, winsome Veronica, who flashes upon you like some tropical bird, with a variety that seems absolutely exhaustless? Born in Germany, on the borders of elf-land, she seems herself half a fairy, with all the airy lightness, the innocent mirth and frolic, and a little of the mischief of that fabled race.

She is not beautiful, at least her features are by no means regular, and her complexion, though clear, is too dark for our Scottish ideas of beauty. But there is so much mind and feeling breathing through her face, so much symmetry and grace pervading her whole person and manner, that you forget all defects, and only feel that she possesses a charm which mere personal loveliness could never bestow. Then too her eyes, not star-like, but wells of living, loving light, have so much soul in their dark depths, that it is impossible to meet their glance with cold indifference

Till I knew Veronica, my mother, sister, and aunt Margaret were my ideals of perfect womanhood. She is entirely different from them all, yet not for that the less lovely or admirable in my eyes. She has not the saintly calm, the quiet repose of my beloved mother; the beauty or sweetness of my darling sister; or the wisdom and dignity of aunt Margaret; but she has something above and beyond them all which is peculiarly her own, which makes its way directly to the heart.

It seemed to me at first, accustomed as I had been to the severity of the nuns, as if the joyousness which came gushing up perpetually from her heart as from an overflowing fountain, was inconsistent with deep religious feeling; but when I expressed this sentiment to my mother she replied:

"My love, there are in the family of

Christ diversities of spirits as well as of gifts. Religion does not change the natural temperament, it only modifies and controls it. As to your cousin Veronica, joyousness and smiles are a part of her very being, and nothing but some overwhelming sorrow can ever repress them. Besides, there is nothing in religion which should drive away innocent mirth, The Christian who, as he looks abroad on this fair earth, can say, 'My Father made it all,' and who feels that all things in time and eternity are his, is the only being in the world who can with any consistency be uniformly cheerful. God is not the God of the dead, but of the living."

"This view of the subject is new to me," I replied. "I have always thought that a proper sense of the vanity and miseries of the world and of our own sinfulness would necessarily make us serious if not sad; such at least has been my experience of holy men and women."

"And did this experience tend to make religion desirable and lovely to you, my dear Kathie? If all mankind were like the holy men and women of whom you speak, would the world be as pleasant to you as it now is? A garment of sackcloth can never clothe a fault or hide a shame; and certainly we cannot atone to God for sin by strewing dust on a sad and disfigured face. No, my child, the man or woman who deals justly and generously by his fellow-creatures, who carries a sunny face and pleasant words into society, and does all in his power to increase the happiness of the world, while he exercises charity for the weak and erring, such a one is most like the great Teacher, and consequently has the best title to the name of Christian. There is a time for all things;

and while seriousness and solemnity become us in the worship of God and in many circumstances of life, a cheerful heart and merry countenance in the performance of our daily duties are equally acceptable in the sight of our Father, who loves to see his children happy. Remember I am not advocating levity or frivolity, with neither of which your cousin can be justly charged, and which have no real connection with that cheerfulness which springs from a heart at peace with itself and with its Maker."

"But dear mother," I said, not yet quite convinced, "you are always cheerful, and Jessie's smiles are the sunshine of my life, and yet there is in your manner a seriousness which leads one always to remember that you look beyond this world for your chief happiness."

Just then the silver laugh of Veronica, followed by one from Jessie, fell on our ears, calling a smile to the lips of my mother as she answered:

"Veronica, my love, must not be judged by our standard, or we should do her injustice. She has been trained up in Germany, under the influence of the teachings of Luther, who from the time of his second conversion was one of the most cheerful of men, and inculcated cheerfulness on his followers as a Christian virtue. She is naturally light-hearted, and has had nothing yet to make her otherwise. May God in his mercy long avert the evil day! Your sister and mother, on the contrary, have been inured to anxiety and care; we are surrounded by strife and bloodshed, and belong to a people who until recently were every where spoken against, feeling that we ourselves or those dearest to us might at any moment be called upon to seal our testimony with our blood.

Do you wonder at the difference? I am glad to see that our dear Jessie feels the influence of Veronica's cheerful and sunny spirit, and is gradually acquiring a buoyancy more suited to her years and natural temperament."

My heart was full, and I could not reply, but as I left the room I silently implored the intercession of the mother of heaven in behalf of the dear speaker; that her sorrows might indeed be over, and the evening of her life calm and unclouded as her virtues deserved.

XII.

Every-day Life.

"I will not shut me from my kind;
And, lest I stiffen into stone,
I will not eat my heart alone,
Nor feed with sighs the passing wind."

JUNE 10.

THE castle seems very lonely since Veronica left us, and no one feels it more, I think, than my brother Robert, who, with all his stateliness and reserve, has evidently found his conqueror, and surrendered at discretion. I dare not rally him, this grave and wise brother of mine, on such a subject; but Jessie and I have many a secret smile at the various pretences which take him so often to Lindisfarn, and the absence of mind he exhibits when at home. The whole thing is so wise and proper, and the choice on both sides so entirely what we could wish, that there would hardly be enough excitement to give it interest, were it not that Veronica is as shy as one of the bright birds whom she resembles, and will only be caught, if at all, upon the wing. But Robert is fully worthy of her, and this her father well knows; so I trust his probation will not be long or painful, though I am sure his persevering spirit would stand the hardest test.

Our domestic circle has been enlivened since Veronica's departure by a relative of hers, who is a cadet of an old and illustrious northern family, and who has recently come from Flanders to Scotland.

Captain Hector Munroe—for so he is called—is about the age of Robert, in the prime of early manhood, singularly frank and ingenuous in character, with all a boy's simplicity and directness combined with the coolness and courage of a practised soldier. His patrimony is small, consisting only of a half-ruined tower near Inverness, and a few acres of moorland; for the family long since lost most of their property by confisca tion; but he is high in favor with Prince Louis of Nassau, and his honorable scars attest his bravery on the field of battle; while, in his conversations with my father, I have been surprised at the wise and statesmanlike views he expresses. Something in his tone and bearing often reminds me of one whom I shall see no more, though in person and temperament they are wholly unlike.

This new comer, I shrewdly suspect, finds our little wild rose a more attractive flower than any that have bloomed in court or palace; and on her part, though I would not if I could, surprise or unveil the secrets of that innocent and loving young heart, I do not think the society of the brave soldier is disagreeable to my sweet sister. I have seen her listen with drooping eye and changing color to his thrilling details of military life, and have felt that the interest with which she heard of the dangers he had escaped might easily be converted into love.

They are suited to each other in age and station, their faith is the same, and they differ just enough to insure perfect harmony of heart and life. But where are my thoughts wandering? Not a word or even a conscious look of love has passed between them, and already in thought I have jumped to the conclusion of the matter.

I fear my friend will say, as she reads this, that two years have changed me sadly; that the Kathie of St. Denis would never have uttered, or even imagined a sentiment like this. Perhaps it may be so, though I doubt whether the human heart is not the same free, fetterless thing in all circumstances until it is crushed; but it must be confessed that life within the walls of a convent and life at Hope Castle in these times are quite different things, and in two years one learns much of the human heart and its capabilities. Indeed when I look into my own heart, and read those around me, it seems impossible that God can have made so wondrous a thing, with its deep and boundless sympathies and affections taking hold of the very centre of our being, only to have it imprisoned and starved in the cells of a monastery or a convent. The mother abbess would tell me that the love thus turned away from earth is all given to heaven. I know that is the theory; but she must allow me to say that, judging from my own observation, it does not seem always to be so. How many vacant, soulless, dejected faces have I seen in the convent, in cases where there was fervent piety and an earnest desire to live wholly for God.

I may as well own that, from the example and silent influence of my dear friends here, I have come very nearly to the belief that the whole system of monastic life in either sex is wrong and unnatural, and that the only acceptable way of proving our love to God is to love our fellow-beings and do them good and make them happy in every proper way. He does not need our services; but the creatures He has made do need them; and if a man love not his brother whom he hath seen, how can he love God whom he hath not seen? I fear my friend will consider me already a heretic; but I must write what I feel, or lay by my pen entirely.

Captain Munroe tells me that Norman Lyndsay is in Germany and Holland, fighting bravely for what he considers truth, and that he is the trusted friend and counsellor of princes. Once I believed him the peer of any man on earth; but now a fatal stain dims the brightness of his character, and the murdered Lord James seems ever to stand between his image and my thoughts, even while I cannot believe him guilty.

In another year my decision, which has long since been made, must be publicly announced, and then the slight tie which now unites us will be sundered for ever. In his own mind it is so already, I know; for he once said to Robert that he could never marry one who was a member of the Romish church, whatever the pleadings of his heart might be; and since leaving Scotland he has written repeatedly to Robert expressing a willingness to take any step which would serve to throw on him the responsibily of a refusal, thus leaving to me the estates of Ormistoun.

This generous proposal, though only what I should expect from him, touches me deeply; but I shall never avail myself of it. While my parents live, it is my wish to remain with them; and since all my wants are supplied by their watchful love, why should I covet the added care and burden of this large and neglected estate? Norman Lyndsay will use it well and nobly, I am sure; and in his hands the interests of the tenantry will be safe. The title and estates of his father, the laird of Rothes, were confiscated in the reign of James V., the father of our queen, and now he is comparatively poor, having retained only the small inheritance of Balderstone, when all besides was lost.

Father Francis will tell me I ought to remember that the church has claims upon me, and that before giving up this property, those claims should be satisfied; but I cannot feel that it would be right to take it from the lawful heir—as Master Lyndsay certainly is—even to throw it into that sacred treasury. I may be wrong; but I am acting conscientiously, and dare not do otherwise.

XIII.

Veronica at Home.

"Beauty is truth, and truth, beauty."

JULY 3.

I HAVE been spending a few weeks at Lindisfarn with Veronica, and every day's acquaintance only increases the love and admiration I feel for this dear cousin. I have done her great injustice in thinking her a being only fitted to sport in the sunshine, and gather honey from the flowers. Beneath her joyousness of manner there is a deep and strong undercurrent of feeling, flowing quietly because of its very depth, and giving a perennial verdure and beauty to her character.

Never have I felt so keenly the miserable emptiness of my own life, as since I have compared it with the rounded fulness of hers. The petted darling of affluence and rank, the delight of her friends, her every wish is anticipated, and her happiness and comfort the study of the household. And yet with all this, she is gentle and unassuming as a child, always forgetting herself in her devotion to others, and causing every member of the household to feel the blessed influence of her kindness and care.

She is literally eyes to the blind, for there are three or four aged and half-blind pensioners to whom she reads the Scriptures daily; and among the poor on her father's estate, she is looked upon as a guardian angel whose coming brings sunshine to their cottages for the whole day. With all her other duties, she has the entire supervision of the schools she has established; knows all the children by name, and distributes rewards in exact proportion to their deserts.

From these various duties she comes into her father's drawing-room fresh, radiant, and joyous, devoting herself to the comfort of her guests as if she had not another thought or care on earth.

And this useful, active, lovely young creature is the one on whom I, Kathie Hope, have dared to look down as inferior to me in moral worth, because forsooth, like the birds and flowers, she gives up all care into the hands of her heavenly Father, and suffers the gladness of her heart to gush forth in songs and smiles. Verily I have received a lesson which will not soon be forgotten.

Lady Ellen complains that I have told her nothing about my uncle or cousin Max. In truth, I have very little to tell. My uncle is a silent, self-centred man, who spends most of his time in his library, busily engaged in writing, or absorbed in thought. He seldom unbends to any one except Veronica, who alone is able to draw him out of his shell, as she playfully terms it. I know he stands high among the leaders of the Reformation as a true patriot, and a man of sound judgment and unbending integrity.

Of Max I would rather not write or think. If he were not my cousin I should call him selfish and unfeeling, with a tendency to low cunning, which it is very painful to witness. He has none of the brilliant qualities which adorn Veronica, but seems rather to have inherited the phlegmatic temperament of his German ancestors.

The father of Lady Dunbar was a nephew of the earl of Arran, who went in early life to Germany, and having married there, settled down, and never returned to his native land. The family have large landed estates in that country, on which Max will probably locate himself, as he dislikes Scotland, and feels but little interest in the great questions that now divide us.

Now that I have touched on this subject, let me make a clean breast in relation to it. Here at Lindisfarn, where I thought myself safe from all external influences, and from Veronica, on whom I have looked as a thoughtless child, I have learned to think more earnestly than ever before, and to ask myself questions, on the right answer to which I feel that my eternal destiny depends. When I hear Veronica's sweet voice singing hymns of praise to the Saviour, in which his love to man, his holy life, and his shameful death on the cross are dwelt upon, the deepest fountains of feeling are stirred within me, and I long, like Mary, to throw myself at his feet, to wash them with my tears, and wipe them with the hairs of my head.

Why is it that this wonderful Personage, who seems so unspeakably precious and near to the believers in the new faith, should in our church be lost sight of as it were, in a crowd of holy men and women, none of whom when in the flesh would have considered themselves worthy to undo the latchet of his shoes? If while he was on earth, the meanest and most sinful always came directly to Him, and found him infinitely more gentle and condescending than his disciples, why is it that now, when as Veronica read to me from her Bible, "He ever liveth to make intercession for us," we may not approach him, save through the intervention of fallible mortals like ourselves?

My mother, sister, and Veronica, all

assert that Jesus does hear and answer their prayers addressed directly to himself, in such a way as to leave on their minds no doubt of the fact. If this be so, then surely such prayers cannot be displeasing in his sight, for we know that the Most Holy can never sanction wrong. If one wished to ask a favor of an earthly prince, one would rather, if he might, go at once to the fountain-head, than to send in his petition through some intermediate source; how much more then, when all that is dear to us in time and eternity is at stake, should we go to Jesus Christ, who is revealed as the one Mediator between God and man.

But it will be said that we are unworthy by reason of sin to open our lips in the immediate presence of God, and must therefore seek shelter behind others holier than ourselves. Is it not true, however, that these very saints were once sinners even as we are, and were saved only through the blood and righteousness of the Redeemer? how then can they have any holiness to impart to us? Moreover, if Jesus loved us while we were yet enemies well enough to die for us on the cross, will he not, when we have become friends, bear with us while we pour out our hearts, with all their wants and sorrows, at his sacred feet? The answer seems to me very plain.

If, as Master Knox says, Christ has finished the work of redemption, brought in everlasting righteousness, and made complete satisfaction for sin, why should I try to add to this finished salvation my own miserable stock of works and penances, which must always be defiled with sin, and utterly unfit to be even named in his presence?

It sounds so sweet, so delightful to

my poor, weary heart, tired with groping after some prop that shall not break beneath me, to hear from those who have tried it, that *simple believing in Christ* does bring rest and peace to the soul. Is it then any wonder that hearing this from those I love and trust, I should long to bring it to the test, and try the same process for myself? I have doubled my prayers and penances, I have gone through the whole catalogue of saints, and lain half the night prostrate before the crucifix, invoking the aid of the mother of heaven—but all in vain; there was no voice nor answer, nor any that regarded. To me, these fountains of supply for the soul's necessities are all empty and broken cisterns, in which is no water.

I have not yet opened my heart to any one here, not even to Veronica, for this is a matter lying between God and my own soul, and I greatly fear being unduly influenced by my friends.

Let it not be supposed from what I have written, that I am about to relinquish the faith in which I have been educated. Ah no; a thousand hallowed memories and tender associations bind me to it by ties which it would almost rend my heart in pieces to break, to say nothing of the friendships, dear as life itself, which must in such a case be sundered. The whole imposing pageantry of our holy church, so fitted to strike the careless mind and impress it with awe and reverence, contrasts so strongly with the naked simplicity of the new faith, that my taste turns from the latter, offended at its unadorned severity. Still, I cannot but feel that all these things are only the externals of religion; the great question still remains, "What does this holy Lord God require of *me*, an individual sinner, in order that I may be fitted to dwell with him for ever?"

This question, and the others I have proposed, haunt me continually, and will not be silenced or disposed of by any process to which I have yet resorted. I am now reading Veronica's Bible, marked by her own hand, and it interests me so much, that I can hardly lay it aside for any other employment. Why this most interesting and wonderful of all books should be forbidden to the common people by our church, seems to me every day more strange, since I see its precepts carried out in the lives, not only of the educated and refined, but among the humblest cottagers on the estate. Some of these poor people who are destitute of all other knowledge, understand so much of the Bible, and seem to derive such strength and comfort from it, that I cannot help feeling as if they must be taught of God, even if the priests do condemn the course they are pursuing.

Only yesterday I had a lesson on this subject, which has made a very deep impression on my heart. Going with Veronica to visit one of her old pensioners, we found her in a miserable cabin, alone and sick, unable to move a great part of the time from rheumatism; yet, when Veronica asked her how she was, she replied with such a happy countenance,

"Ah, my leddy, I've been all day sitting under his shadow with delight, and his fruit is sweet to my taste."

When Veronica expressed sorrow on finding her suffering so much, she replied,

"Indeed it's naething but just an answer to prayer. Ye see, my leddy, I've lang prayed to be made more like my Saviour; and since this is his means, I've naething to do wi' the choosing of them. That's the end I seek, and I maun leave it to his wisdom to take his ain way wi' me. I'd rather suffer than sin, ony day."

If such are the fruits of the study of God's word, why should it not be placed in the hands of every human being?

XIV.

Changes in Prospect.

"Coming events cast their shadows before."

AUG.

THE last letter from France pains while it does not surprise me. I was well aware that Father Francis, the mother abbess, and indeed all the sisterhood, would regard what I have written as a hopeless defection from the truth; and yet I could not resolve to keep back from them the conflict through which my mind was passing. They seem to me to have reasoned badly when they conclude that because I am studying the Bible, therefore I must of course be led astray. If as I still believe, the truth is essentially with the Catholic church, then surely she has no reason to fear or shun the strictest investigation, as it can tend only to confirm the faith of her children. But if it be otherwise, God forbid that I should any longer continue to walk in darkness when the light of life is shining all about me.

Their proposal that I should revisit France for a season, that I might see and converse with the bishop and the holy fathers, is very kind, but I cannot accept it for two reasons. The first is merely personal to myself, and need not be repeated here; but the second is imperative, and my friends in the convent would be the first to admit its validity.

Our dear young queen is coming back to her throne and her kingdom; and in making up a list of her ladies, Lord James Stewart has done me the honor to include my name among them. I did not suppose it possible to obtain my father's consent to this arrangement;

but he has the most sanguine hopes that on this occasion some agreement may be brought about between the two contending parties of Catholics and Protestants, and is willing to contribute his mite towards this desirable event. The offer has therefore been accepted in fitting words of gratitude, and in a few weeks, or as soon as possible after the arrival of the queen, I shall leave my quiet, peaceful home for the splendor and gaiety of a court.

To say I am glad at the prospect of becoming a personal attendant on Mary of Scotland, would be to express very feebly a sentiment which possesses and absorbs my whole soul. And yet it is not, I am sure, the love of change, or a wish to shine in the circles of the gay, or mere worldly ambition, that attracts me. But ever since my childhood I have felt a romantic interest in our fair young queen, exiled while still an infant from her native land, and subjected to the control of proud and imperious strangers. When afterwards I saw her at the Louvre, looking among her attendant maidens like an angel surrounded by mortals, my heart was filled with love and devotion to her cause, and every year since that time has only strengthened the feeling. I am certain that many trials await her in this land, which must seem to her so cold and inhospitable after her own sunny France; and if my poor efforts can do any thing to add to her comfort I would willingly yield up my life in this service. There is also another inducement in the fact that at Holyrood I shall again enjoy the ministrations of priests of my own religion. I have no wish to visit the confessional, for I have learned to confess my sins to God alone, and have little faith in the absolution given by mortal man; but it will be pleasant once more to attend the services of the church, as I was so long accustomed to do, and to know that those around me sympathize in my feelings and belief.

One circumstance in the coming changes gives me sincere pleasure. My uncle, Sir James Dunbar, is appointed one of the members of the privy council, and will reside with his family in Edinburgh at least half the year. This will bring them into the court circle; and as Robert and Veronica are betrothed, I shall see this dear brother more frequently than I had dared to hope.

Last month I reached my legal majority, and as soon as possible afterwards met the trustees of the deceased Patrick Carr, formally to refuse the hand of Norman Lyndsay, and thus to relinquish all claims to the Ormistoun estate. The trustees stared upon me in amazement, deeming me probably a demented lassie; but wisely supposing that argument would be thrown away in such a case, did not try to turn me from my purpose. Master Lyndsay, to whom the estate very properly reverts, is therefore no longer a "landless laird," as since the confiscation he has been, but a rich and powerful heritor; and if ever permitted to return in peace to Scotland, will have wealth and influence in abundance.

But common fame speaks of him as seeking on every occasion the very forefront of the battle; and if he did not bear a charmed life he must ere this have fallen beneath the Spanish sword. There are rumors afloat which clear him from the stain of murder, and point to a very different quarter for the guilty parties; but all concerning that event is involved in darkness and mystery, and I have little hope that it will ever be otherwise. Revenge is a virtue in this distracted country, and there are few, except among the adherents of the court, who look upon the deed with any strong feeling of abhorrence. Indeed, it seems passing away from the mind of the people, though the feelings it engendered still remain.

I forgot at the time to mention a little incident which occurred while I was at Lindisfarn, and which may interest my friend. We were all invited to dine with a Mr. Morison in the vicinity of my uncle's house, and during the evening a white-haired gentleman, whose venerable appearance we had admired, was introduced to me as Master MacNeal. He made many inquiries concerning my residence in France, and when told that I was in the convent of St. Denis, exclaimed:

"St. Denis! that surely is the convent where poor Isabel Douglas, in the first bloom of youth and beauty, buried herself for ever from the world. Poor lassie! So fair and so unfortunate; my heart always aches when I think of her."

"Is she there still?" I inquired, for something in his manner interested me greatly.

"I have never heard of her death, young lady," he replied, "and nothing else can open for her the convent doors. My poor Isabel!"

I asked him if he knew what name she had assumed on becoming a nun.

"Oh yes. I was present when she took the veil, and heard her addressed as sister Agnes before she disappeared for ever from my sight."

I was startled at this announcement; and as my thoughts ran back over the period of my residence in the convent, I could not doubt that the sister Agnes whom I had loved so much, and who was mother, sister, friend, all in one, was the same with this noble Scottish damsel of whom Master MacNeal had spoken. A thousand little circumstances flashed across my mind, bringing conviction along with them. Why was this never known to me before? Why, when listening so indulgently to my praises of bonnie Scotland, did sister Agnes never even hint that it was her native land as well as mine? There is a mystery about this silence which I find it impossible to solve.

Master MacNeal spoke of a severe disappointment which nearly broke the heart of the beautiful Isabel, and drove her from the gay circles she was so fitted to adorn into the seclusion of a convent. What this was he did not say, and as I could not bear to have the heart-history of one I love so dearly publicly discussed, I would not inquire. When I remember the sweet patience, the constant cheerfulness, and the utter forgetfulness of self that always marked the character of sister Agnes, it is hard to believe that the storm of sorrow has passed over her, withering the blossoms of her life and bearing away all its hopes.

I trust sister Agnes will pardon me, should her eye ever meet these lines, for thus alluding to the past, concerning which she has been so profoundly silent. Nothing would tempt me to give her pain, but in writing this for my friend, I have been in the habit of thinking aloud, and cannot easily learn another lesson.

XV.

Mary Stuart at Holyrood.

"The palace of pageantry crumbles away;
Its beauty and strength are marked by decay,
And a voice from the desolate halls of kings
Cries, Put not your trust in perishing things."

SEPT. 9.

I AM now at home, making hurried preparations for an immediate return to Edinburgh, whither I went with all the family, to meet and welcome our long-absent sovereign to her native shores. Yes, she has come back to us at last, our anxiously expected and desired queen, whose return is the bow of promise shining athwart the clouds that have long obscured our skies.

The day on which she expected to land proved so dark and foggy, that the ship could not safely approach the shore; so it remained quietly in the offing, with the queen and her attendants on board. A few boats, with some of the chief dignitaries of the state on board, went out during the day to the vessel; but most of the strangers who thronged the city waited with what patience they might for the clearing of the skies. The morning of the twenty-first of August dawned clear and bright as our hopes, and we all hastened to Leith harbor, where the vessel lay, eager to catch the first glimpse of our liege lady as the ship came proudly up to the shore. On leaving the deck, when her foot touched the shore she stopped for a moment, clasped her hands, and raised her beautiful eyes to heaven, while the air resounded with shouts and acclamations on every side.

A white palfrey, the best that could be obtained in the emergency, with rich housings that nearly swept the ground, awaited the queen, and as she rides with perfect grace, every eye was fixed upon her with admiration and delight. Horses were also provided for the numerous retinue of the queen; but though they were of an inferior quality, and some of them wretched hackneys, still it was very bitter to me to witness the smile of contempt with which they were regarded by the proud ladies who followed in her train, and who were accustomed to the noble and richly caparisoned steeds of Paris. But this small source of annoyance was soon forgotten when the cavalcade started.

On the queen's right hand rode Lord James Stuart, her half-brother, and formerly prior of St. Andrew's, and on her left Lord Hamilton, duke of Chatelherault, Mary's nearest relation, an aged nobleman who has some time since retired from public life. Lord James is one of the handsomest men in Scotland, and very popular with the Protestants, as he is strongly suspected of having embraced their faith. He is also the idol of the populace, and was loudly cheered even in the presence of his sovereign. The procession was long, consisting of the nobility who followed the royal cortége, the members of the Privy Council and officers of state, the Romish priesthood and the reformed clergy, who for once agreed to walk, or rather ride together; and lastly, a motley crowd of the lower classes, who shouted a welcome to the daughter of their guid king Jamie to the throne of her ancestors.

When the queen and her retinue swept through the arch of the ancient palace of Holyrood, and vanished beneath its frowning portal, the waiting crowd were invited to the great square of the city, and there feasted at the expense of the magistrates.

In the evening the halls and saloons of the old abbey of Holyrood were thronged by the noblest and fairest of Scotland's dames, both maids and matrons, the bravest of her warlike sons, and the most illustrious of her scholars and statesmen. All were alike eager to be presented to their youthful queen; and as one of the maids of honor elect, it was my privilege to occupy a place in the inner circle nearest her majesty.

From the moment of her appearance, I had eyes and ears for nothing else in that vast assembly. First in grace and beauty, as in place, Mary Stuart stood amid the crowd like some bright particular star; like that too moving calmly in her own high orbit, apparently unconscious of the admiration she excites.

Shall I try to paint my impressions of this most beautiful of women, whose charms are celebrated throughout Europe? The attempt seems like presumption; still it shall be made. Like the opal, her face is constantly changing as the light of the soul shines through it, and each expression seems lovelier and more charming than the last. Her figure is slightly above the middle size, fashioned so perfectly as to exhibit alike the extremes of grace and majesty. One moment she is every inch a queen, regal and dignified in bearing as becomes the name she inherits; the next she is wholly the woman, all sweetness, smiles, and fascination. Her hair of deepest auburn, has a golden lustre in the sun, and melts in the shade into a dark chestnut. Her eyes of dark gray, languid and yet brilliant, speak directly to the heart. Her complexion is exquisitely fine and fair, in which the wild rose of her native hills and the lily of France blend in such beauty. But why do I dwell on her features, when, in spite of their perfection, they are not her principal charms?

It is the wondrous union of feminine ease with royal dignity, of courteous affability towards the meanest and poorest of her fellow-creatures, with the evident consciousness of all that is due to herself and her exalted station; this it is that wins every heart, and makes Mary of Scotland the most beloved, as she is the loveliest, of queens.

She wore a robe of black velvet, fitting closely to her person, a falling ruff of the finest Flanders lace, and a cap of the same material, drooping low on the forehead, and surrounded with a double row of pearls of the purest water, while a single string of the same priceless gems encircled her fair neck. Such was her attire; far more simple than that of any of her attendant ladies, whose gorgeous dresses gave additional splendor to the scene.

From my post of observation, I saw that the sternest barons and preachers of the Reformation—with the exception of Knox, who was not there—who have always denounced the regent and her court, now crowd round the young queen, as eager to obtain a smile from those sweet lips, or a bend of that graceful head, as the most devoted of her followers. There seemed to be a glamour over the eyes of all, as if for one brief evening the hate of party and the fierce clashing of creeds had resolved to sink their differences in cheerfulness and good fellowship.

At length my turn came for presentation to her majesty, who stood in the centre of the large apartment, with her four Marys nearest her person, and a circle of courtiers about her, most of whom had come with her from France. As I knelt before her and kissed her hand, she raised me, saying graciously,

"Thou art welcome, Kate"—for so she will always call me—"to my family and my heart. It is not the least of thy merits, in my eyes, that, as I have learned, thou dost know and love la belle France. I trust we shall be able to make thee so happy here that thou wilt forget thou hast ever known another home."

So saying, she presented to me the bright young girls who bear her name and are first in her regards, adding with her own sweet smile,

"Ye must love one another, and let Mary Stuart feel that there is at least one charmed circle into which jealousy and strife cannot enter."

"Our only strife shall be, your grace," replied Mary Carmichael, who seemed the most brilliant of the group, "which of us shall best love and serve our royal mistress."

A look from the queen was the only reply; but it was so full of expression, that words could have added nothing to its meaning.

My mother and sister were presented by my father, and received with such winning courtesy and kindness, that Jessie exclaimed as she came back to my side,

"She is indeed a queen for whom one might live or die; for once report has fallen below the truth."

Such seems to be the universal opinon with regard to her majesty, even among those most opposed to the church to which she belongs. Lord James, or the earl of Murray, as he has been created, is devoted to his royal sister; and Morton, Ruthven, and Kirkpatrick, stern and dark-browed as they are, feel her influence, and join the circle at the palace on every fitting occasion. Master Andrew Melville has been several times to Holyrood to wait upon the queen in behalf of his brethren; but John Knox has never yet entered her presence; and Robert tells me he never will unless, in the discharge of his duty, he should be called upon to make some direct appeal to her conscience.

He is now preaching in one of the churches of this city, and has an immense congregation, who hang on his lips as if he were the dispenser of life or death to their souls.

XVI.

Truth Confronting Royalty.

"He shall stand before kings."

MAY, 1562.

I HAVE been to confessional and heard mass constantly since coming to this city, and yet my heart is ill at ease, and harassing doubts incessantly pursue me. Nearly every thing about me, all that I see and hear in the palace, tends only to increase them. Religion here does not seem, as at Hope Castle and Lindisfarn, to be a principle planted in the heart, and from thence influencing all the actions and feelings; but rather an outward observance of tedious and unmeaning ceremonies, which make no impression on the heart and life, unless it be to make one a fanatic or a bigot.

My beloved mistress is kind and gracious as ever; but I cannot help seeing that even in her case her belief has no practical influence on her heart or life and that when she has gone through with the external duties demanded of her by Father Sebastian and by her station, she comes back to the world with a sense of relief, as if her treasure and her heart were both there. God forbid that I should judge one whom I love and revere so much; but it seems as if faith in God had little power to comfort her, for she is always, when in private, either immoderately gay, or looking back with tears of regret to her residence in France, and contrasting it with the trials which surround her here.

It is not yet a year since she landed on our shores, and already the conflicting elements that were hushed for a few short months are again busily at work, producing discord, strife, confusion, and every evil work. The courtiers, many of whom are French, look with polite contempt on what they term our coarse northern manners; and the feeling is fully returned by my countrymen, who talk of the frippery and folly of mounseers, fiddlers, and dancing-masters, with a bitterness which they take no pains to conceal.

Many of the priests outrage public sentiment by shameless profligacy of life, declaring openly that all things are lawful for them; and that with the rich, money will procure absolution for any kind of crime, so that unlimited indulgence may be had by them if they are willing to pay for it. Even the queen's confessor does not hesitate to sell indulgences privately, though I am certain his royal mistress would be indignant if she knew the fact.

On the other hand, Master Knox and the other preachers inveigh from the pulpit in the strongest terms against what they call the papistry of the blinded queen and her courtiers and ladies, and call on the people to come out from among them and be separate and touch not the unclean thing. The queen, who fears and dislikes Master Knox, has several times invited him to the palace; but he has been here only once, and then his denunciations of popery, and his warnings of wrath to come, wearied and disgusted her.

To me, I confess, there was something grand in the sight of that noble old man, unawed by the splendors of a court, the terrors of a throne, or what most men would find it more difficult to resist—the charms of a young and lovely woman, whose beautiful eyes, fixed upon him, seemed entreating him to spare her. He is reported to have said elsewhere that she was "in sooth a most goodly and fair creature to behold; and that if she might be plucked out of the hands of Satan, she would be worthy to stand by the side of Esther, as a nursing mother to the church." But in her presence, though he was careful to observe all the etiquette due to her station, it was evidently the queen of Scotland, not the woman, to whom he bowed; and he did not hesitate to denounce the dress, amusements, and follies of the court in the strongest terms. For a while the queen heard him patiently, assuring him that, though she loved the Catholic church and would never leave it, still she would never have any of her subjects persecuted for their belief, but was resolved to promote toleration to the utmost of her ability.

"But it is strange, methinks," she

added with spirit, while her cheeks glowed and her eyes sparkled like brilliants, "that your queen should have less liberty of conscience than the lowest of her subjects. The poorest hind may enjoy his belief in peace; while my privacy is broken in upon, the religion I hold sacred denounced foully, and my person and friends insulted with impunity in my very presence. Is there nothing in all this, Mr. Preacher, of which I might justly complain?"

"Assuredly, honored madam, if your rank in life were private, it were but right that your belief should lie between God and your own conscience; but he hath seen fit to place your highness as it were on an eminence, where your influence is widespread for good or evil, and must needs affect the eternal destinies of many souls."

"According to your showing, Master

Knox," replied her majesty, "it is a misfortune to be born a queen, instead of the good thing men commonly regard it. I must, perforce, be glad that others do not agree with you in this opinion."

"The opinion of the world is with me a light matter, madam, when called upon to speak the words which God puts into my mouth. He bids me tell you that the belief of your majesty becomes a matter of public interest, insomuch that it ought to be right; or if wrong, that it should not be paraded to the scandal and injury of the realm. This it is which gives to me and others the right of remonstrance when we see the interests of Christ's kingdom endangered by the flaunting of papacy in our very faces."

The queen rose with dignity, and taking the arm of Mary Seyton, turned to leave the room, saying as she did so,

"Since Mary Stuart may not call the apartments of her palace her own, or enjoy her privacy when she lists, she can at least retreat, leaving the intruder master of the field, and wishing him joy of his victory over a crowd of helpless maids and matrons."

Most of the ladies in waiting followed the example of their mistress; and when only two or three pages were left in the room, I went up to Master Knox, who was standing quietly near the window, and touched his arm. Then in a low tone, for several pairs of inquisitive eyes were fixed upon me, I inquired for the health of dear aunt Margaret.

Mechanically, as it seemed, he began to answer, "The Lord be thanked, she is well;" when suddenly starting from his reverie, he exclaimed,

"Kathie Hope here, in this den of papistry and iniquity? Child of my old friend, what doest thou here? This is no place for one like thee."

"You forget, dear sir," I replied, "that I also am a member of the church you denounce so strongly; and therefore, in your estimation, blinded and lost."

"Blinded indeed. But, daughter, thou art a child of many prayers, and though Satan may desire to have thee, that he may sift thee as wheat, thou shalt not always be left in his hands."

I know not how it was, but something within forced me to say, with a rush of blinding tears,

"I own I am very unhappy, and do not see one step of the way before me. Who will lead me into the truth?"

How tenderly that stern man laid his hand on my bowed head, saying with the gentleness of a woman,

"Dear child, the blessed Saviour, who styles himself the good Shepherd, will himself teach you and lead you into all truth; he will feed you in green pastures, and make you lie down beside still waters, if you will only look to him and trust his guidance. Will you not do this?"

"Alas, I know not where to find him," was all I could say."

"He is not far from any one of us, Kathie, and the wish to find him, proves him already very near you. Every desire of your heart, however imperfectly breathed, reaches his gracious ear and touches his loving heart. Read the Bible, child; study his character in the gospels, and then thou canst not choose but love him. Thou hast a Bible, I trust."

"When at Lindisfarn," I answered, "Veronica insisted on my taking hers, and I have kept it, though reading it always makes me more restless and dissatisfied with myself and every thing about me, and I have often resolved I would study it no more."

"Beware of such a resolution as that, Kathie. Sooner might the man sick unto death reject the physician, because his remedies were unpleasant to the taste. The Bible is God's voice to man, and if its perusal makes you unhappy, it is because you are far astray, and not yet willing to come back. Read it with humility and prayer, and be assured that then the entrance of those blessed words will give you light. But I must be gone, for I would not that the mis-proud minions who now throng this old pile should have occasion to bid me depart."

My heart was very full, and I could only say, "Pray for me," as he prepared to leave the room.

"God forbid that I should sin against

my own soul and thee by neglecting so plain a duty. And now, my daughter, farewell. May he who protected Daniel in the lions' den, and the three children in the fiery furnace, bless and keep thee, and open thy mind to the truth."

Master Knox has not been to the palace since; and her majesty, with all her usual gentleness, is so incensed at what she terms his insolent rudeness, that she has no wish for a second interview.

Father Francis, the abbess, and the nuns will, I am sure, believe me mad or infatuated; still I must confess that I have come to the firm resolution of studying the Scriptures for myself, excluding, as far as possible, all human opinions and prejudices, and shutting myself up in my chamber, so that alone with God, his voice may perchance reach my poor troubled heart, and direct me in the way of life. So far as I know myself, I have no will about the matter, and only want to know what is truth; and like the publican of whom I read in the Bible, I too would say, "God be merciful to me a sinner."

There is no one about me to whom I can go for counsel; for my young companions, full of mirth and gaiety, would look upon my feelings as moonstruck madness; and the royal Mary, with all her kindness and forbearance, has little sympathy with gloom or sadness. I often long to be at the castle with my mother and sister, though I doubt whether, even if I were there, it would be possible for me to overcome my reserve so far as to let them see what is passing in my heart.

Oh for one hour with Veronica—dear, straightforward Veronica—who, without waiting for permission, walks directly into your confidence, and uses it so wisely and tenderly that you cannot help blessing the intrusion. I know she would feel for me, and with all her childlike joyousness she is almost as wise as my father, or even Master Melville himself, and would be sure to direct me right.

Has not every one felt, in looking abroad, that there are two kinds of mirth in the world? The one kind is fleeting and vain, like the crackling of thorns under a pot—an empty noise without solidity or heat, and soon over: the other is the overflowing of a heart at peace with God and with conscience, and is ever fresh and perennial as the fountain from which it flows. Veronica's cheerfulness is of this kind, and seems wholly independent of external circumstances. But she is now far away, on a visit to her friends in Germany; and as Robert has accompanied her, there are none about me but comparative strangers.

XVII.

Queen Mary Among her People.

Peace greatness best becomes; calm power doth guide
With a far more imperious stateliness
Than all the swords of violence can do,
And easier gains those ends she tends unto."

SEPT. 4.

I AM now at my dear home on a short visit, while the queen and the court are staying for a few days in Perth and its vicinity. She has made a royal progress through the North, visiting the palace of Linlithgow and Stirling Castle—places in which her infancy was spent—and passing one day at Falkland, where her unfortunate father breathed his last.

While we were at Stirling Castle, her majesty had a very narrow escape from death; and a death so fearful, that the thought freezes my blood with horror. The evening had been spent in revelry and mirth, and the queen retired to her room at a late hour, and was soon buried in a profound slumber. The lady in waiting that night followed the example of her mistress, and all was still, when a page in the antechamber was wakened by a thick smoke filling the apartment. He called Lady Maxwell, who, on entering the chamber of the queen, found the curtains of her bed all on fire. The flames had communicated with the bedclothing, and in a moment more our royal mistress would have been beyond the reach of help. As it was, we found it difficult to rouse her, half-suffocated and bewildered as she had become with the heat and smoke.

For a few moments all was confusion and dismay; but as soon as the queen came fully to herself, she took the direction of affairs, and by her presence of mind, the flames were speedily extinguished, and order restored before the seneschal of the castle had become aware of the danger.

Master Maitland of Lethington, secretary to her majesty, came running in when all was over, and had to take much laughter and many jests in consequence from the four Marys, who were full of mirth and merriment.

Soon after this the court came to Perth; and here, in the cradle of the Reformation, to my great sorrow the Protestants made a public demonstration against the religion of the sovereign; ridiculing the priesthood, the mass, and indeed every thing belonging to the church. It was an insult to an unoffending queen who, whatever her private belief may be, has always treated her subjects with marked courtesy and kindness—an insult offered in cold blood and by previous agreement; and she felt it deeply, changing color and biting her lips to restrain the words that were ready to rush forth from her indignant heart.

When, on the next day, the provost and members of the city council waited on her to welcome her to the ancient city, she heard them with quiet dignity, but in her reply could not refrain from a few touches of sarcasm, which no one knows better how to use than Scotland's Mary. The pompous but well-meaning dignitaries were sadly humbled by this reception of what they believed to be a most moving speech, and left the royal presence with slow step and dejected countenances. But though in this instance the queen betrayed her wounded feelings, she very rarely does so; for she excels in that species of kingcraft which consists in finding a way to the hearts of all others by smiles and kind words, while her own is carefully hidden from view.

I think her majesty feels every day more keenly the difficulties of her situation. The Catholic priests accuse her of timidity and time-serving because, from kindness of heart as well as motives of prudence, she refuses to adopt the strong measures they urge upon her. On the other hand, the reformed preachers are indignant at the liberty granted her to have mass celebrated in her own chapel, and exclaim against her blind devotion to the idolatries and superstitions of the Romish church. They are highly displeased also at the action of the court party in settling the provision for the ministers of both churches. The Privy Council have determined that the ecclesiastical revenues shall be divided into three parts, two of which shall go to the ejected popish clergy, and the remaining third be divided between the court and the Protestant ministers.

Master Knox exclaimed to my father, when told of this division,

"If the end of this thing be happy, my judgment fails me. I see two parts freely given to the devil, and the third part shared between God and the devil; and it will go hard with the devil, I think, if in the end he do not manage to get it all."

Very recently the same great man said in the pulpit,

"One mass is more painful to me than if ten thousand armed men were landed in any part of the realm, of purpose to suppress the whole religion; for in our God is strength to resist and confound any multitude, if we only depend upon Him; but when we join hands with idolatry, there is no doubt that God's pres ence and defence will leave us; and what then shall become of us?"

One may see from this the feeling that prevails among the Protestants, who are by far the strongest party, and the thorny path which our beloved sovereign is called to tread. From my soul I pity her, and my love for her is the strongest tie which now binds me to the Catholic church. Yes, it is even so; the scales have fallen from my eyes, and I cannot help believing that the truth of God is with Luther, Knox, and those who adhere to their doctrines; but though no longer tossed about with doubts, I am far from having found the peace of which others speak. My heart seems to grow harder and more wayward every day; and even the love of Jesus has no power to melt it.

Since coming to the castle, I have conversed freely with my dear mother, and her counsels and prayers have been an unspeakable comfort to me. She says she has never since my return from France doubted that a faithful God would, in his own time, bring back her wandering child, in answer to the prayers that have ascended to him on my behalf.

My father and Sir James Melville are again in England, on a mission of state to Queen Elizabeth; and Jessie, who is betrothed to Major Hector Munroe, though kind and good as ever, can think of little else besides her own happy prospects. How lovely she is, this sweet young sister, in the flush of early womanhood, with a future bright as love and hope can make it spread out before her.

On a more intimate acquaintance, I believe Hector Munroe to be worthy of the heart he has won, and higher praise than this I could hardly bestow. Prince Louis of Nassau, younger brother of the prince of Orange, urges his return to Holland; but the earl of Murray, who wishes to raise troops for the defence of Scotland in whom he can confide, desires him to remain at home and take a command in the army here; and as my mother and sister second this wish, and a commission has already been sent him, he will undoubtedly decline the proposition of the prince.

To-morrow the court returns to Edinburgh.

XVIII.

Looking Backward.

"Praising what is lost,
Makes the remembrance dear."

AUG. 2, 1563.

ONLY two short years have fled since I came to Holyrood, an inexperienced girl, believing every thing to be just what it seemed, and ready to lay down my life for the young and beautiful queen who was in my eyes only a little lower than the angels. Two years' experience of the splendors of a court has disenchanted me; and though I still dearly love my too indulgent mistress, I cannot shut my eyes to the acts of imprudence and error which will, I fear, prove fatal not only to her influence but her happiness. Unlike what we hear of her great rival Elizabeth of England, she suffers the woman to overcome the queen, and where her affections are concerned takes counsel of feeling rather than judgment. The earl of Murray, her half-brother, has more influence with her than any other courtier, and I cannot but believe that he might if he so willed, save her from many a wrong step by a few words of brotherly counsel and admonition; but instead of this, he seems blind to all her failings when with her, and actually encourages her in caprices which may shake the very foundation of her throne. With all his fair seeming and professions, I have doubts concerning this gallant nobleman, who is the second personage in the kingdom, and if his royal sister were removed, would be the first. It seems to me cruel and treacherous to abuse the confidence which the queen reposes in him, by suffering her to take one wrong or imprudent step which his utmost efforts could prevent. But I am treading on dangerous ground, and will turn to other subjects.

My father was appointed a commissioner of the kirk last year; and as he has long lived for others far more than for himself or his own ease or emolument, most of his time has been devoted to the duties of his office. Jessie too has left home, having been since her marriage, which took place in December last, on a round of visits to the friends of Captain Munroe, in the south and west of Scotland and on the continent. Thus deprived of husband and children, my dear mother found the deserted home too lonely for her, and came early in the new year to Edinburgh, on a long visit to dame Margaret Knox, who for a year past has been entreating this favor.

It was the wish of the great reformer

to live in the humblest manner consistent with neatness and comfort, both from inclination and as an example to the poor of his flock. But Lord Ochiltree, the brother of aunt Margaret, insisted on providing them a house, together with the plenishing, and in consequence they are pleasantly and even nobly lodged. But a truly Christian spirit reigns within the dwelling, and the poor outcast meets there as cordial a welcome and is made as truly at home as the most favored child of fortune.

Some of the happiest hours of my life were spent in that peaceful and hospitable home, when seated at the feet of my mother, with my hand clasped in hers, I listened with deep interest to the conversations between her and aunt Margaret on the love of Christ, and the blessedness that awaits the believer in a future state.

Sometimes Master Knox would come in, and naturally taking the lead of the discourse, tell us of the advancement of the good cause in other lands; of the persecution of the Huguenots in France, or the brave stand taken by the Flemings against their proud oppressor, Philip of Spain; or leaving the externals of religion, he would discourse most eloquently of the worth of the soul, the price paid for its redemption, and the means necessary to secure its salvation. These sources of enjoyment were far sweeter to me than any I tasted in the circles of gaiety and fashion, and unlike them, these left no sting behind.

The enemies of the great preacher accuse him of being a woman-hater, and of wishing to deprive her of all independence of thought and action, since he deems our sex incapable of judging or acting wisely. From what I have heard him say to my father, as well as from his published works, I know he thinks it neither right nor proper that women should occupy stations of public trust and authority; but in private life I have seen nothing that would indicate a dislike to female society. There never was a kinder husband, a more courteous host, or a more considerate and forbearing friend, save where he considers the interests of religion at stake. In such cases he forgets every thing but that he is God's ambassador, and is truly a son of thunder in denouncing idolatry and wickedness.

In the course of the royal progress through the north last year, the queen had a private interview with Master Knox at Lochleven, in which she exerted all her wonderful powers of fascination to soften his heart and secure his friendship. She even condescended to request him to assume the office of her private monitor, promising him that she would never be offended at any boldness he might use in the discharge of his duty.

But even this delicate flattery failed to soften or silence him. He assured her grace that as long as she upheld the mass and other kinds of idolatry in the kingdom by her example and influence, so long he must pray and preach against her, no matter what his feelings towards her personally might be.

"It will avail nothing," he said in conclusion, "to point out your grace's private faults while this public scandal and wickedness goes on, injuring souls and putting in peril the best interests of church and state. If your grace would judge for yourself, and not look at every thing through the spectacles of the priests, you would see that this realm hath been made free by God himself, and can never again by any means be brought into bondage to Rome. I warn your highness, that on whomsoever this stone shall fall, it will grind him to powder."

Since that time the queen will hardly suffer the name of the preacher to be spoken in her presence, for she both hates and fears him; saying in her own private circle that she feared the prayers of John Knox more than ten thousand men brought against her in the field. And yet, with all her fear and dislike, she respects and esteems this man for his unconquerable boldness in speaking what he believes to be the truth, without regard to the fear or favor of man. Whatever his enemies may say of his belief or principles, there is something morally grand and sublime in the attitude of such a man, standing up before the nation in avowed opposition to the sovereign and her court, unawed by threats and unseduced by flattery, in simple obedience to the dictates of conscience. Can the religion be wrong which produces such fruits?

After the return of the queen from her northern expedition, many months passed away in quiet happiness, unmarked by any important political event. There are those, and I confess myself among the number, who tremble at the increasing influence of the earl of Murray over the counsels and actions of his sister and queen. It would almost seem, from the ease and certainty with which all his plans and wishes are carried out, that the Lord James is king of Scotland, and Mary Stuart only his subject. I trust his professions of attachment to her are sincere, and that he has really her interests at heart; but it is far less easy to reconcile his actions with this supposition than with one directly opposite.

One extremely painful incident varied the monotony of court life last year, which I will state briefly. The poet Chatelard came in the queen's train when she left France, and has remained in Scotland since. He was a gentleman of good family and fortune, being a lineal descendant of the Chevalier Bayard, the man "*sans peur et sans reproche.*" He had long been in the habit of addressing his royal mistress in verse in the most extravagant terms of passionate admiration; but accustomed to every species of flattery, and looking on it as part of his profession, she only smiled at his extravagance and forgot it as soon as heard. These smiles however were fatal to Chatelard. They nourished his presumptuous hopes, and led him to acts of audacity which gave her majesty great and just offence, and led her to reprimand him severely before her maids of honor.

The leniency of Queen Mary was thrown away on the infatuated poet. In the vain hope of justifying his conduct on a previous occasion, he contrived to introduce himself into her chamber at night, and when commanded by her to leave the room instantly, refused to obey; on which she called for assistance. The earl of Murray was at hand, and came instantly. Of course the bold daring of the mad poet could no longer be concealed; and the requisite authority having been procured from Edinburgh, he was tried at St. Andrew's, where the court was then staying, and condemned to death. He died like the enthusiast he had shown himself throughout the affair, refusing to see a priest, and exclaiming with his last breath:

"Farewell! loveliest and most cruel princess whom the world contains!"

The honor of the queen was vindicated, but her heart was sorely wounded by the necessity laid upon her, and for several days her depression cast a gloom over the whole court circle; but her natural buoyancy of spirits is so great, that no event has power long to overcome it. It is well for her that this is so, since otherwise, amid all the trials that beset her path, she would be constantly unhappy.

XIX.

John Knox at Holyrood.

"I will not speak
With bated breath and honied words, to suit
The ear of greatness, when the God I serve
Bids me proclaim his message in broad day,
And on the housetops, though the wealth of Ind
Were offered me in guerdon. What I hear
From those dread lips that spake on Sinai's mount,
That will I utter though the world in arms
Were ranged against me."

JULY 15, 1564.

MORE than a year since, my father and his friend Sir James Melville were sent to England, to consult with queen Elizabeth concerning the marriage of our sovereign, who is the lineal heir of the English queen, provided she should die without posterity of her own. She professed great interest and kindness, but would only recommend her own rejected suitor, the earl of Leicester. So as it would hardly comport with the honor of our liege lady to take up with the cast-off favorites of her sister queen, the attempt came to nothing. Meanwhile, many others were proposed, some Catholic princes and noblemen, and others Protestant; and though it cannot be doubted that the royal Mary has decided preferences of her own, she is resolved, for reasons of policy, to be guided as much as may be by the wishes of England in regard to the matter, in order that her right of succession to that throne may not be endangered.

Master Randolph, who is in the interest of Elizabeth, came recently to St. Andrew's, where the queen with her favorite ladies was staying privately for a few days, in order to find out from her own lips what were her real sentiments on the subject of marriage.

The queen treated him with great kindness, inviting him every day to her own table; but when he attempted to introduce matters of business, she would say to him playfully,

"I sent for you to be merry, and to see how like a bourgeoise wife I live with my little troop, and you must needs interrupt our pastime with your great and grave matters. I pray you, sir, if you be weary here, return home to Edinburgh, and keep your gravity and great embassade till the queen goes thither, for I assure you you shall not find her here, nor know I myself where she is become. Ye see here neither cloth of state, nor such appearance that you may think a queen is here, nor would I that you should hold me to be the same at St. Andrew's that I was at Edinburgh."

Thus bantered out of his purpose, Randolph was fain to relinquish it for the time, but he renewed it on every occasion, till in the frankness of her heart, the queen satisfied him fully of her intentions if possible to follow the wishes of Elizabeth in her choice of a husband.

On her return to the city, hearing that great opposition was being made by the preachers of the Reformation to her marriage with a Catholic, she sent for Master Knox, and desired another interview with him.

He came accordingly, accompanied by Lord Ochiltree, brother of his wife, and many others, but none came with him into the queen's cabinet, save Erskine of Dun, a man who occupies the debatable ground between Catholics and Protestants. Her majesty, who had seemed troubled and unlike herself all the morning, no sooner saw him enter than she exclaimed,

"Surely never was prince so ill-treated and sorely perplexed as I have been. I have borne with you, Mr. Preacher, in all your rigor of speech against myself, my uncles of Guise, and my religion. I have sought in every way to win your favor, and have even offered to give you audience and hearing whenever it pleased you to admonish me, and yet I cannot be free from your abuse. By all the saints, but this is too much, and I am resolved to be avenged."

Never before had such sharp words been heard from those beautiful lips, but Master Knox stood wholly unmoved, and answered quietly,

"It is true, madam, that your grace and I have had divers controversies, in which I never yet perceived that any offence was taken against me. If it shall please God to deliver your grace from the bondage of error in which you have been trained, and to teach you the new doctrine, you will, I trow, find nothing unfriendly in my preaching. Out of the pulpit, I trust none can accuse me of too much plainness of speech; but there, madam, I am not my own master, but must speak that which I am commanded by the King of kings, and dare not, on my soul, flatter any one on the face of all the earth."

The queen listened with flashing eyes and swelling bosom, and when he had ended, impatiently exclaimed,

"But what have you to do with the marriage of your sovereign? What are you in this realm, that you should dare to dictate in such a matter?"

"I am a plain man and your subject, madam, born within this commonwealth; and though neither knight, baron, nor earl, yet has God made me, however unworthy I may seem in your eyes, a profitable member of the same. When I see things that seem to me wrong, it appertains to me, no less than the nobility, to forewarn of such things as may be hurtful to the state, for both my vocation and my conscience crave of me plainness of speech, and therefore it is that I speak to your grace as I have. If the nobility of the realm consent that you shall be subject to a Romish husband, they do what in them lies to renounce Christ, to banish the truth from Scotland, to betray the cause of freedom, and in the end, to secure small comfort to yourself."

During this speech the queen was greatly excited and shed many tears, and Erskine of Dun tried to comfort her grace, by assuring her that all the princes of Europe would be proud of an alliance with a princess of her beauty and excellency. But his words made no impression, and it was truly painful to see our royal mistress in such a tempest of passion. The great reformer, however, never changed countenance, and answered in his usual low tone,

"Madam, I speak it as in the presence of God, whose unworthy servant I am, I never did delight in the weeping of any of God's creatures; yea, I can scarcely bear the tears of mine own children when my hand corrects them; but seeing I have given you no just cause of offence, but have only spoken the truth which my office demands, I must bear, though unwillingly, your majesty's tears, rather than hurt my own conscience or betray this commonwealth through my silence."

This speech incensed her majesty to such a degree, that she commanded him to leave the apartment instantly, and await her pleasure in the antechamber.

I left the presence soon after, and going into the outer room, saw there a large company of courtiers, pages, and ladies in waiting, laughing and ridiculing the preacher, while all the Protestant lords stood aloof, fearing to share his disgrace, save Lord Ochiltree, who stood by and conversed with him. In this situation Master Knox was calm and composed as in his own room in the High-street; and after a while, turning to the group of splendidly dressed and smiling ladies, he said to them,

"Oh, fair ladies, how pleasant would this life of yours be, if it could ever abide, and then in the end you might pass into heaven in all this gay attire! But alas, the knave death cometh whether we will or no, and when once his arrest is upon us, then the worms will be busy with this tender flesh, and the soul I fear will be so startled that it can take with it neither gold nor silver nor precious stones in its flight."

The consternation with which such an address would be received by a gay court circle, may easily be imagined. There was a great fluttering among them, but to their relief and joy, Erskine of Dun came in, and warned Master Knox to depart, which he did immediately. The queen urged the Privy Council to devise some punishment for the bold reformer, but they persuaded her to overlook this offence, and so the storm passed over; but she has never forgiven it, and I believe never will.

A few weeks since, the earl of Lennox, whose countess is aunt to the queen, came to Scotland, and very soon after his son, Lord Darnley, followed him, there having of late been some talk about him as a suitable husband for his royal cousin. He is well made, and so far as thews and sinews go, a marvellous proper man; but I like him not, for his goodly frame seems to me like a stately house utterly void and destitute of tenants. But he is well skilled in all the manly accomplishments valued in courts; and more than every thing else, our mistress evidently favors his suit, so I doubt not it will carry the day. But while peasants and inferior personages can make their choice and marry without obstacles, a queen's love is subject to many and vexatious delays. But in spite of obstacles, all here is mirth and merriment in the court circle; plays, masques, and other amusements are the order of the day, and the queen gives herself up to the society and pleasure of Lord Henry, who on his part is the most devoted and obsequious of cavaliers.

Indeed, he may well be proud of the influence he has acquired over the most beautiful woman of the age, besides that the marriage is far above any reasonable expectations he or his parents could have entertained.

Immediately after the ceremony, the royal party are to pay several visits to some of the principal nobility, and then I hope to have the pleasure of going to Lindisfarn, where Robert and Veronica are expected daily to arrive from their long stay in Germany. I am anticipating much from this visit, not only in the delight of seeing those I love once more, but because my soul is thirsting for Christian counsel and communion, which, since my mother's return to Hope Casle, I have never enjoyed. I cannot go to the confessional or to hear mass at the queen's chapel, and dare not brave her displeasure by attendance on the established kirk, so I have no spiritual nourishment, and consequently make little progress in the knowledge of God.

True, my father and uncle are often at Holyrood, and we have frequent opportunities of communication, but they are public men, with hearts and minds full of great interests, and however kind, would have little sympathy with the feelings of a girl. But to Veronica, my sweet, hopeful sister cousin, my heart opens as naturally as flowers to the sun. I need her sympathy and wise counsels, and thank my God for sending her to me just when her presence seems most necessary.

XX.

A Royal Wedding.

"Ye blazing stars of gems and gold,
What aching hearts ye mock ;
Strong marble walls do ye not hold,
Sword, poison, axe, and block.

"Ye lowly born, Oh covet not
One right the sceptre brings ;
The honest name and peaceful lot
Outweigh the pomp of kings."

AUG., 1565.

WOULD that I held the pen of a ready writer, so that I might properly describe on paper the gorgeous ceremonial we have recently witnessed. The marriage between Mary Stuart and Henry Darnley, with which all Europe is ringing, was solemnized in the queen's chapel at Holyrood on Sunday, the 29th of July. John Sinclair, bishop of Brechin, performed the ceremony according to the rites of the Catholic church, though the bridegroom is in reality a Protestant.

Never, surely, since the bridal of the first pair in the garden of Eden, has a nobler looking couple been seen upon the earth. Lord Darnley, though hardly twenty, has a person and appearance inferior to none in manly beauty and dignity of manner; and I need not repeat what is known to all the world, that Queen Mary is more beautiful than even a poet's dream of beauty.

The festivities must have seemed to her poor and tame, compared with the sumptuous elegance of the French court; but they were such as Scotland has never before witnessed, though in consequence of the troublous times armed men stood even beside the altar.

The royal bride, in a flowing robe of black, with a wide mourning-cloak, was led into the chapel by the earls of Lennox and Athol, who first led her up to the altar, and then retired to bring in the bridegroom. The bishop having united them in the presence of a large concourse of lords and ladies, three rings were placed on the finger of her majesty, the centre one being a rich diamond. They then knelt together, and many Latin prayers were said over them, which the priests probably understood much better than most others in the chapel.

When all was over, Lord Darnley kissed his fair bride, who looked most lovely even in that unbecoming dress; and then, as he is not a Catholic, he left her in the chapel to hear mass. On reaching her own apartments, she threw off her mourning garments, thus signifying that as she was again a bride, she now laid aside her mourning for her first husband. In observance of an old custom in royal weddings, as many of the lords as could get near enough to her person were permitted to assist in her toilet by each taking out a pin. She was then committed to her ladies, by whom she was dressed with a splendor never before exhibited since coming to this country.

After this, the company assembled in the ball-room, and dinner was soon served, at which Lord Darnley appeared in his royal robes, making a fine show for the multitudes who were looking with eager interest on his lordship's movements.

In the evening the state apartments were thrown open for the first time, and the hours flew rapidly away in dancing and merriment. The French servants of the queen had the arrangement of the rooms, and the halls of Holyrood never before presented such a scene. Hundreds of lights flashed from the tapestried walls; wreaths of the choicest flowers were twined around the columns; strains of voluptuous music floated through the halls, while perfumed tapers and burning censers filled with incense made the air heavy with fragrance.

With even more than her accustomed grace—brightest and most beautiful where all were bright and lovely—Mary Stuart glided among her high-born guests. No shade of sorrow dimmed that transparent brow or clouded that radiant smile; the whole scene was one of congratulation and rejoicing. The tone of the queen was no less bland and courteous when she addressed the gloomy Morton or the stern Lyndesay, than when speaking to her own loved and chosen associates.

When the newly married pair took their places in the centre of the large apartment, to lead off in the brawl or dance, every eye was fixed upon them in admiration and delight. Never since the old abbey became the habitation of kings did a nobler looking pair grace the ancient halls of Holyrood. Taller and more stately than any baron present, excepting James Earl of Bothwell, Lord Darnley looked noble and kingly, as his robe of ermine swept the ground; and our royal mistress was absolutely dazzling in her gorgeous robes, flashing with diamonds, rubies, emeralds, and other precious stones. But so rich were the royal pair in personal advantages and attractions, that the splendor of their dress seemed only a fitting accompaniment, and was no more marked by the beholder than is the golden halo which surrounds the heads of Raphael's saints, while we gaze upon the sublime sweetness of their pictured faces. Dark-browed men smiled upon her, and even Lyndesay exclaimed in my hearing,

"In sooth, she were a most fair creature, if her mind did but match the glories of its mansion."

But in the midst of all this mirth and splendor, what was it that made thoughts of the grave, of judgment and eternity, perpetually intrude upon my mind, in spite of all my efforts to drive them away? At such moments, the lights would grow dim around me, the music died away in a sad wail upon my ears, and I turned with a sick shudder from the offered attentions and flatteries of the gay gallants by whom I was surounded.

Once during the evening the queen, who chanced to be near me, observed the shade of sadness which unconsciously overspread my face, and said kindly,

"What is it, my Kate, that brings a cloud to this fair brow, and dims the sunshine of this laughing eye? Thou hast a kind and leal heart, my girl, and will, I am sure, rejoice with me in one of the few hours of happiness I have known in Scotland. Mary Stuart loves better far to look on a smiling lip than a wet eye, even if it were a stranger's, much less that of one whom I love as I do thee, my Kate. Cheer thee then, I pray thee, for thy queen's sake."

Oh why is not this fascinating woman as wise and firm and true as she is kind and lovely? Then would she be in truth worthy of the devotion she inspires, and poor Scotland, under her rule, might almost realize the fabled age of gold. But what can be expected from one educated, as she has been, in the profligate court of France, and under the tuition and example of Catharine de Medicis, the crowned Nemesis of Europe?

From most of the priests too, who have her confidence, she can learn nothing but lessons of treachery and deceit; for though I regret to say it, yet the truth is that most of them seem alike destitute of the fear of God and man.

There can be little doubt that one of the main causes of the downfall of the Romish church in this realm was the extreme wickedness of the priests, by which the common people were outraged and driven to desperation. The ministers of the reformed church, on the contrary, are a strict, temperate, God-fearing set of men, whose example may safely be followed by their flocks; and in this respect alone the gain to the cause of pure morality is immense.

I have had several interviews lately

with Father Ignatius, a priest who came from Rome to Scotland by the way of Paris, where he learned from the bishop my spiritual danger, and set himself most zealously to bring back the erring sheep to the true fold. The arguments he used, and which once I thought unanswerable, now seemed hardly worthy of an answer, they were so puerile and weak, and I was enabled to maintain my ground without yielding an inch, so long as he confined himself to the infallibility of the church, the supremacy of St. Peter, the deadly sin of schism, and other similar topics.

But when, finding his arguments thrown away, he changed his ground, and painted the sorrow and distress of Father Francis, the mother abbess, Sister Agnes, and even of my friend Lady Ellen, at what they regard as my fatal delusion, my eyes filled in spite of myself. Father Ignatius, seeing the conflict within me, took courage, and pressed upon me entreaties, commands, and even threats, till my Scottish blood was fairly up; and I assured him that, having once tasted the sweetness of reading the Bible and thinking for myself, I should never relinquish the privilege but with life itself. He left me in a storm of passion which knew no bounds, even of courtesy, and since then has not honored me by a look.

XXI.

Domestic Happiness.

"Oh, link but one spirit that's warmly sincere,
That will heighten your pleasure and solace your care;
Find a soul you may trust as the kind and the just,
And be sure the wide world holds no treasure so rare."

SEPT. 7.

I AM once more at Lindisfarn, once more sunning myself in the light and warmth that like an atmosphere surround this dear Veronica. Robert too I find greatly changed for the better since his marriage. The influence of a wife has made him more frank and genial in manner, and he is now a most delightful companion, so kind and intelligent and well informed on all subjects of interest.

Jessie and her husband are now here, with a little Hector. who in the opinion of his fond parents, unites all the graces and virtues of his progenitors on both sides in his tiny person. It is charming to witness the joy and pride with which the young mother bends over the infant king, whose wishes are a law to all about him, or the tender reverence with which she regards him as a being intrusted to her by God himself to be trained up for him.

Major Munroe is strongly attached to the earl of Murray, who, with his other rich gifts, possesses in an uncommon degree the power of winning all hearts, and considers it a misfortune for Scotland that his birth shuts him out of the position he is so calculated to fill with honor, namely, that of king. He says the situation of the kingdom, torn as it is by two great opposing factions, and filled with turbulent barons and lords, requires a more powerful hand than that of a woman to hold the reins of government securely.

It is not difficult even now to see on the horizon the cloud scarcely bigger than a man's hand, which threatens to overspread the land, devastating and laying waste our hopes. The queen sees it not; for accustomed from her infancy to flattery and subservience on the part of all who approach her, she cannot be made to believe that any one could be found hardy enough to oppose her will by the strong hand until the reality is upon her. Loving my royal mistress as I do, I cannot but hope that the danger may yet be averted; but there are voices and mutterings in the air on every hand, and I tremble for the result.

Most of her foreign attendants have gone back to France, as their presence here occasioned so many jealousies and broils in the court; but her private secretary, David Rizzio, an Italian by birth, still retains his office in spite of the dislike with which Lord Darnley and other noble lords regard him. He has great influence with the queen, who thinks herself bound in honor to protect him, since she imagines that his faithfulness in her service has brought upon him this odium and disgrace. On the other hand, many believe, and with show of reason, that if the favor with which her majesty regards him were less evident, he might retain his place without difficulty, and be quite overlooked by the proud barons whom he now delights to brave. I have seen Ruthven, Lyndesay, and others, cast upon him looks which froze the blood in my veins, they were so full of savage hatred; but Rizzio seemed quite unmoved by them. If he knew more of our rugged northern temper, which is most dangerous when in stillness it bides its time, he would hardly look upon it so quietly.

Meantime, while strife and tumult and rumors of wars fill and agitate the earth, here in this lovely and quiet retreat we walk in the sunshine and breathe the fragrance of flowers and hear the singing of birds, with none to molest or make us afraid. The grounds about Lindisfarn are full of beauty, and they have been laid out and kept in order by a gardener who came with the family from Germany, six years since.

I find it pleasanter here now than on any former visit, for Max is away permanently, and Veronica, as "lady of the hall," sheds the light of her buoyant spirit on all within the sphere of her influence.

"Do you know," she inquired of Robert one evening as we were enjoying together a glorious sunset on Ben Lomond, "what plan I have been forming recently?"

"That little brain is always busy forming plans to make somebody better and happier," he replied with a smile; "further than that I am unable even to guess."

"In return for that compliment, Robert, I must certainly make you a sharer in my project, especially as I shall be obliged to call on you for help in carrying it into effect. You remember when we visited the German Christian village, how delighted we were with the order and neatness of the poorest cottages, making them seem almost like a little paradise, and how painful to us was the contrast with the huts of our own tenantry at Lindisfarn. On inquiry I found that these results were produced by a regular system of supervision, together with rewards for the most deserving, given at the close of the year by the heads of the community. The best and most industrious and tidy wife and mother or mistress of a family, received as a reward of merit a pair of horn spectacles and a new spinning-wheel, or a large copy of the sacred Scriptures.

"Now we need in our cottages something like this to stimulate the housewives to a more thorough and cheerful discharge of their duties. I am sure our Scottish women would be second to none as wives and mothers if they only could be brought to understand their duties, and had some increased facilities for preserving order and comfort in their households. As it is, I do not wonder that they are discouraged."

"But how does my household fairy propose to remedy this state of things?"

"By establishing a kind of club, to which all may belong who are really desirous of improvement. This club shall have an annual meeting in some part of our own grounds, at which time rewards shall be distributed by one of us to all who, during the year, have made decided progress in cleanliness, order, and industry. The children of the most deserving shall be admitted into the school which I mean to establish near the glen head, as that will be the most central place on the estate."

"Your plan, my dear wife, seems to me wise and practicable if you can find the right instruments in carrying it out; but what can I do for you in the way of assistance?"

"I shall not need to tell you that, Robert, if you remember the neat and pleasant cottages on your father's estate at the Castle, all the result of his own kindness and care, and then contrast them with the comfortless cabins about us here. You know my father leaves every thing in your hands, and you can make what changes you think best, with his full sanction. Of what use will it be to try to teach neatness and comfort to the inmates of a sheeling filled with smoke that has no way of escape but by the door; with a floor of earth, unglazed windows, a roof gaping with crevices, and only one large apartment in which all must sleep, without regard to decency or comfort?"

"I understand you, dear Veronica," Robert replied, "and have long felt ashamed of our own luxuries when I have contrasted them with the utter destitution of the poor peasantry about us. I thank you for calling my attention to the subject, and setting me the example of caring for these neglected ones, and will gladly do any thing in my power to carry out your wishes in their behalf."

"If all that is necessary were done at once," said Veronica, whose wise little head seems to look on all sides of a question, "the good effects would I fear be lost, at least in part, since so great a change would only confuse and bewilder the housewife. She must first be taught how to keep clean a pine floor and glass windows, how to manage the fire on a hearth with a chimney for the smoke. and in what way to arrange beds in a sleeping-room, before she will be able to appreciate the value of these things. Let the good women first be taught to make the best possible use of what they have, and as they learn to discover what is wanting, let it be supplied, till their dwellings are made snug and comfortable."

"But how is all this to be done? Desirable as it is, I cannot consent to give you up to the work, even if you had not already quite too much on your hands."

"You give me too much credit," was the smiling reply, "if you think me capable of teaching all that these poor women must learn. Ah no, dear Robert, this thing is much better arranged, I assure you. The widowed mother of little Donald Ferguson, in whom you felt so deep an interest, is a devoted Christian and a very intelligent woman, with a thorough knowledge of domestic affairs, which she acquired while living at Strathbogie in the capacity of housekeeper. She has only Donald with her, and will gladly do any thing in her power to assist in the plan I have proposed to you, for she feels as we do in relation to this whole subject. I propose giving her the pretty little cottage near the keeper's lodge, rent free, and for a small sum she will devote her whole time to the work of instructing the members of the club, who are to meet at each other's cabins in rotation every week, and her visits to them at their own homes will be frequent, that she may give practical lessons there. I shall uphold her authority by my presence as often as possible, and in this way we may hope to bring about a permanent and most desirable change for the better in the condition of the poor."

"It is like you, my Veronica," said Robert, with a tender reverence in his tone, "and that is the highest praise I can bestow upon your plan. You may depend on my assistance to the utmost extent of my ability."

As Veronica belongs to a class with whom *doing* always follows closely after *intending*, her plans were speedily carried out, and before I left Lindisfarn for Hope Castle the good effects were already visible.

If her life is spared, there will in a few years be a class of peasantry at Lindisfarn who will show the world of what the Scottish tenantry are capable when neatness, industry, and good order are grafted on their natural firmness, intelligence, and piety.

XXII.

The Uses of Beauty.

"God, the undiluted good, is the root and stock of
beauty,
And every child of reason drew his essence from that
stem."

"It is a part of the nature of man to be ever thirsting after the beautiful."

OCTOBER 30.

I HAVE seated myself to relate, before it is forgotten, the substance of the following conversation, which took place a few days since between Veronica and myself, and which I have preserved, because I have heard Lady Ellen express sentiments so similar to those of my sister, that I thought it might give her some pleasure.

My brother had been proposing to give a dinner party to some military friends who have returned from the Low Countries recently; and after he left the room, Veronica playfully advised me to be sure and dress as becoming as possible, since we were about to meet some of the heroes whom the war of the Netherlands has rendered famous.

I replied with some asperity, I fear, that it seemed to me foolish and wrong for immortal beings to waste time and thought on the adornment of bodies which were so soon to be laid aside in the grave.

Veronica replied with her usual sweetness, "If you mean that it is wrong to have this our first or chief thought and care, I agree with you entirely. But dear Kathie, these bodies, of which you speak so slightly, were fashioned by God himself, and are master-pieces o. creative wisdom and skill. If it was not beneath the great Maker to bestow upon them such exquisite skill and care, surely it cannot be beneath us to take the best possible care of his work, and to adorn it so as to make it pleasing and attractive in the eyes of others. Why should man and woman, the glory and crown of the creation, be wholly outdone and thrown into the shade by insects and birds and blossoms, by shutting out from their lives all grace and beauty as to design or coloring in the draperies they wear? Our Saviour pointed his disciples to the lilies of the field, and assured them that the more than kingly splendor with which they were arrayed was the work of the Creator, while they were the passive recipients of his taste and his goodness. He who made this earth so full of grace and beauty; who painted the clouds which make our sunsets so glorious, and gemmed the sky with myriads of flashing stars, and planted the most exquisite flowers in obscure spots on which the eye of man has never yet rested—surely He must be not only a lover of beauty, but himself the very essence and source of all beauty, physical as well as moral. Indeed, my sister, I think that Christians are apt to undervalue the beauty which is external and strikes the senses only, as being beneath their notice, when in fact it is one form of truth, and just as much the work of God's hand as the soul or spirit of man."

"The idea is new to me," I replied, "for I have always seen the men and women who aspired to become saints making themselves look as hideous and disagreeable as possible, and believed this a necessary part of religion."

"And were you not in consequence disgusted and repelled by such an unlovely exhibition? It is nothing but a caricature of religion, and scares other people away from it. I do not wonder that when men of the world see religion, or what passes for such, transforming bright and pleasant people into gloomy and disagreeable-looking ones, they think it a misfortune to become a Christian, and shun it as they would some prevailing epidemic."

"But you know," I said, "that our church teaches the doctrine that the body is our greatest enemy, and that we can only become holy by mortifying its desires, and subjecting it constantly to painful penances."

"There is one grain of truth concealed under all this mass of error, Kathie, and that is the fact that we must bring all our passions and propensities under the control of reason and religion, if we would ever hope for holiness and heaven. But the body, by God's grace assisting us, may be made a helper in the good work, instead of a hinderance; and if it is, as the apostle tells us, 'the temple of the Holy Ghost,' ought we not to reverence and carefully cherish it?"

"You may be right in this idea," I replied, "but it does not follow that we may innocently adorn the body with ornaments and gay apparel after the manner of the world, does it?"

"In this, as in every thing else, dear sister, wisdom is profitable to direct; for I believe that the woman professing godliness cannot run to the extreme of fashionable folly without placing her salvation in fearful peril. But I think it right for our sex, as well as the other, to dress in accordance with the rank and station in society which God has assigned them, and I cannot believe it wrong to study what is becoming to our style of face and feature in the selection and arrangement of the articles we wear. Never certainly was there a richer dress than that ordered by God for the high priest to wear when ministering before him, studded as it was with gems of untold value, and more unique and costly than the robes of kings. Look at Solomon's temple, built after a pattern given directly from heaven, and tell me where on earth could a building be found richer and more gorgeous? Every thing too in the temple service was splendid and imposing beyond any thing known to the polished and luxurious Greeks and Romans of that age.

"But you will say these things belonged to a peculiar dispensation. I grant that, and only speak of them because to me they prove that ornament and beauty cannot in themselves be wrong, or they would never have been sanctioned by the Holiest in his own special service."

"But do you not think, Veronica, that the love of dress is calculated to foster vanity and pride in our own hearts? And if this is so, can it be innocent?"

"Certainly not, if this is a necessary or even a general result. But, Kathie dear, do you not suppose that the mendicant friar who boasts so loudly of his humility, is prouder of his tattered robe and belt of rope, than our Robert of the fitting dress in which he appears so well? And may not the heart of the nun swell as high with spiritual pride—the most offensive of all in the sight of God—under the haircloth vest and garment of serge, as if still arrayed in the silks and velvets and jewels she once wore? Vanity and pride are our bosom foes, and must be constantly watched and guarded against, but in my opinion they depend for subsistence far less on externals than many suppose."

As I looked on the fair speaker, I could not but feel that she was herself a striking illustration of the truth of her own remarks. Lovely and graceful in person, and always dressed richly and tastefully, she was a charming study for a painter; but when once her toilet was made, she seemed to have no more thought of her own appearance than the bird whose rainbow plumage flashes like brilliants in the sun with every movement. Even the infant in its mother's arms, as its embroidered robes swept the ground, was not apparently more unconscious of its outward adorning than my sweet sister.

From her my thoughts went back to the sisterhood of St. Denis, with their stiff black habits and frightful looking headgear of linen, and their countenances which so plainly expressed, Come not nigh unto me; I am holier than thou; and I was convinced that Veronica was right. Pride is a vice that can flourish in the most barren soil, and find aliment quite as readily in deformity as in beauty.

"You have conquered, as usual," I exclaimed. "I see that it was only another form of spiritual pride to which I was on the point of yielding. I am certain that my mother and sister agree with you on this subject; for while they dress with simplicity, nothing could be more tasteful or becoming than their ordinary attire. I am naturally fond of dress and display, and when my darkened heart could find no rest nor peace, something whispered that not until I should learn to mortify the pride of the flesh by the plainest possible style of dress, could I hope to find the blessedness I was seeking. In my situation at court it was impossible to do this, so I despaired of help or comfort; but you have taught me, dear Veronica, that the finished work of Christ does not need to be patched out by the fig-leaves of our own righteousness. Thanks, under God, to your teachings, my sister, Jesus has made me willing to be indebted to him for every thing, in this world and the next, without even one little penny-weight of my own to cast into the scale."

I have repeated this conversation because, as I look back on my acquaintance with the friend for whom I write, I am convinced that she too has found the golden mean between the love of display on the one hand, and improper negligence in dress on the other; and that, even in the bosom of the Catholic church, she is led by the same Spirit into a union of views with my Protestant friends on this subject. When I compare her, moving in the midst of that gay and wicked court pure and uncontaminated, with my dear friends in Scotland, I feel more than ever before the truth of the inspired declaration that the Highest "is no respecter of persons: but in every nation he that feareth God, and worketh righteousness, is accepted with him."

XXIII.

What Came of the Dinner Party.

"Trust me, 't is a soul above your scorning,
With God's image stamped upon it, and God's kindling
breath within."

Nov.

IT is now past midnight, and I am sitting alone in my room, trying to bring my throbbing heart into subjection, and to collect my scattered thoughts; but the effort is almost in vain. All that has taken place within the last few hours seems like a confused dream. I cannot believe that I have once more heard the voice and looked into the eye and clasped the hand of Norman Lyndsay; and yet it is really so.

But let me state things as they occurred. I had dressed for dinner, and was reading in the library, when Veronica came to me, all smiles and radiance, begging me to go to the withdrawing-room, as some of the guests had arrived, and neither Robert nor herself were just then at liberty to go to them. The request struck me as rather singular, but I prepared at once to comply with it, and went with her through the long corridor, thinking once upon the way that there was a strange flurry in her manner, usually so self-possessed and unconscious.

As we entered the room, I found only one gentleman in it, who was standing with his back to the door, looking out upon the landscape. Something in the tall, powerful frame, and the well-poised head, made my heart beat strangely; but when he turned and advanced towards me, I was so astonished that I could only stand still and gaze upon him without uttering a word. I had so long looked on Norman Lyndsay as dead to me, and persuaded myself that we should never meet again on earth, that I could not at once admit the idea of his actual presence in the flesh before me.

But it was the same face, furrowed by time and care, and bronzed by constant exposure, but with the same thoughtful, penetrating glance of the eye, the same kindly smile and winning manner, so full of manly dignity, yet frank and genial as that of a brother. In his presence it was impossible to remember that I had ever believed aught against him—ever doubted him for a moment. Without a word of denial, the accusation fell to the ground, and his innocence seemed proved beyond a cavil.

He addressed me as an old friend, and without any appearance of constraint, while I could only answer him in monosyllables, unable to give utterance to one of the many thoughts that filled my heart and crowded up to my lips. After a while Veronica came in with Jessie, and then Robert and Hector followed with several other guests, so that the conversation soon became general, and to my great relief the entrance of little Hector with his nurse gave me an opportunity to retire to a distant window-seat with them.

Jessie went into the dining-room with Colonel Lyndsay, and sat by him during dinner, chatting familiarly as became their long friendship, while from my seat by a boisterous west country laird, I could only hear broken sentences of their conversation on subjects which seemed of deep interest to both.

After dinner, when he came back to the withdrawing-room, he was so surrounded with gentlemen listening eagerly to his account of the Spanish war in the Netherlands, that it was long before I had an opportunity to exchange even a word with him. At length, however, he made his escape, and seating himself by me, inquired in a tone of kind regard,

"And has my friend Kathie been happy in Edinburgh all these years, or does she sometimes weary of the splendors of a court?"

"I still love my royal mistress dearly," I replied, "but the glamour is no longer over my eyes which at first made the palace and its inmates so enchanting."

"May I venture to ask what has disenchanted you?"

"Experience and reality," was my answer; "two stern but useful teachers. I have been behind the curtain, and can never go back again to the beautiful dreams of my youth."

"Pardon me," he said with a manner of deep interest, "but I wish very much to know whether those dreams have given place to others equally perishable, or to that which alone is reality?"

I knew well what he meant, but something seemed to make it impossible for me to answer him frankly; so I evaded the question, and replied with a levity I was very far from feeling,

"Oh, you must not inquire too closely into the nature of dreams; they are usually of flimsy material, and quite unworthy of your notice."

This foolish speech was no sooner made than I would have given worlds to recall it; but it was too late. He looked pained, but made no reply, and soon after entered into conversation with Veronica, leaving me to the solitude I had so richly deserved.

I could not endure the thought of

his departing from the house with the impression I had left on his mind, but resolved to watch my opportunity, and at all hazards to make an apology for my flippancy, and answer his question frankly. Accordingly when, in the course of the evening, I found him standing near me, without giving myself time for reflection, I said to him,

"Colonel Lyndsay, you must have thought me rude and heartless in the extreme in evading your question as I did. Forgive me; and if you have any interest in the answer, I promise to give it frankly and truly."

Surprised, but evidently pleased, he replied with great gentleness,

"There is nothing to forgive, dear young lady, unless it be the doubt you have just expressed that I should feel an interest in all that concerns you. As the daughter and sister of my best friends, you have an undoubted claim upon me, even if there were no other."

I was alarmed by this allusion to the past, and hastened to say,

"When I saw you last, I thought nothing could ever induce me to forsake the faith in which I had been educated; but the silent example and influence of those dearest to me induced me to examine the Bible for myself, that I might find, if possible, the causes of the difference between them and the members of my own church. You know where it is said, 'The entrance of thy words giveth light.' It penetrated even my darkness; and now I trust I can humbly say, 'Whereas I was blind, now I see,' though still imperfectly and indistinctly."

"Thank God," he exclaimed fervently; "and permit me to thank you also, dear young lady, for the confidence you have manifested in me. But has not this change in your feelings affected the comfort of your position at court? The Catholics are not wont to look with complacency on those whom they regard as recusants from their faith."

"In the palace of Holyrood," I replied with a smile which I could not repress, "little is said or cared about creeds or belief. If one is but willing to assist in making the present life enjoyable, one is seldom questioned about her opinion of another. Through the kind indulgence of the queen, I have been allowed to absent myself from the mass and confession, though I have not ventured to request permission to hear Master Knox, as I would gladly do. But three months of every year have been spent at Hope Castle and here; and I need not tell you how much of strength and comfort I have gained from the society of the dear friends in both these happy homes."

"They are indeed the excellent of the earth," he replied, "and judging from my own experience, Scotland has few such homes of which to boast as Hope Castle and Lindisfarn."

Here our conversation was interrupted, and Colonel Lyndsay soon departed leaving me in a strange whirl of conflicting emotions. Not a word had been said to disprove the accusation against him, yet I believe in his innocence just as firmly as if it had been proved by a hundred witnesses. But it is late, and I must lay aside my pen.

XXIV.

Hours of Sunshine.

Nov.

I HAVE often sought my room to pour out, through this medium, my doubts and cares and sorrows into the ear of an earthly friend, sure of the sympathy which is so dear to every human heart, even when I knew she could not understand the conflict through which my soul was passing. Now I come with my joy, for my heart is so full of gladness that it must flow out in words, though tears will start at the recollection that years may elapse ere the happiness of the past week can be renewed.

But I forget that I am talking in riddles, and will try to be more explicit.

For a few days after my first meeting with Colonel Lyndsay, I did not see him again, as he was absent on important business with my brother and other gentlemen; but immediately on his return, he came to Lindisfarn. Veronica was absent attending to duties connected with her schools, and to my great chagrin, I was left alone to receive him. His manner was so full of frank and brotherly kindness, that it soon placed me at my ease, and for some time we chatted on indifferent subjects, until, seeming to remember that the time was fast passing away, he suddenly exclaimed,

"Miss Kathie, I have long wished for an opportunity like the present, to say a few words to you in relation to a matter which has given me no small anxiety and distress."

I knew what he meant, but could not smooth his way by word or look; so he went on:

"The will of your friend and my kinsman the laird of Ormistoun was, I think, both impolitic and unjust. As such I have always regarded it, and before leaving Scotland the last time, did all in my power so to arrange the business that it should be impossible for you to deprive yourself of that which the owner certainly intended to bestow upon you, though he unwisely clogged the gift with conditions which rendered it of no value."

"You are wrong, Colonel Lyndsay," I replied eagerly; "I have no claims, and never could have any, on the generosity of my godfather. You are his legal and rightful heir, and to me it would be robbery of the basest sort to have availed myself of his mistaken kindness."

"I do not need it," he answered with a smile that had more of sadness than mirth in it; "I can, with the blessing of God, carve out a livelihood with my own good sword, while at the same time I am doing something for the cause dearest to me on earth. It would have pleased me, when far away, to think of you as the lady of Ormistoun, blessed yourself in blessing others, while following the example of your excellent parents in making the wilderness about you blossom as the rose."

"That picture never could have been realized by me," I said in a voice choked by emotion; "for I am blind and ignorant myself, and need constant teaching and guidance. Besides this, when I leave Holyrood, it will be to return to Hope Castle and devote myself to my parents in their declining years. But it is vain to speak of what might have been. The estate has passed for ever from my possession, and it is in the right hands, for which I thank God most fervently. You cannot, it seems to me, throw off the responsibility without sinning against your own conscience and the souls of the scores of immortal beings intrusted to your care, as God's steward over them."

I was frightened at my own boldness, but he answered gently,

"You are not probably aware that my honor is pledged for a speedy return to the Netherlands, where that illustrious prince, William of Orange, is leading the forlorn hope against the treacherous and cruel Philip of Spain? I love and honor the prince above all living men; and if for any selfish interest I leave him in this time of extremity, may God forsake me in the hour of my utmost need."

Awed by the solemnity of his manner, I yet ventured to inquire,

"But since you must go, could not some trusty friend be found to take your place in the management of the estate and the care of the tenants during your absence? It has long been suffering, if I am rightly informed, for lack of the master's eye and hand."

"Blessings on you for that thought," he exclaimed; "it makes the path of duty plain before me. My friend Captain Farquhar of the dragoons, one of the best and noblest of men, was badly wounded at the battle of Bergen ap Zoom, and has not yet recovered from the wound. He will be unable to go back with me; and as he is alone in the world, and poor in purse, I am sure that for my sake he will take the place of superintendent at Ormistoun, and do all in his power to instruct and elevate the peasantry there. Should I die abroad, the estate will then go into the right hands; and in case of my return—but there will then be time enough to settle all that. And now, my friend, that this affair is happily arranged, will you suffer me to speak of another which concerns me yet more nearly?"

I trembled without knowing why, as I answered in a tone as steady as I could make it,

"You can say nothing to me, I am sure, which it would pain me to hear, and I have entire confidence in you."

"How can I thank you as I would for that assurance, my dear young lady; it almost renders unnecessary what I was about to say. I need not tell you that when I went to the Continent, my name and fame were darkened by an accusation which, though abhorrent to my whole nature, I could not then either deny nor disprove without bringing misery and disgrace on some who were innocent of the crime. After weighing the subject in my own mind as impartially as I could, I came to the conclusion that it would be less injury to the good cause for me to bear the odium, however undeserved, than to throw it where it belonged, and I have acted accordingly.

"But a few weeks since, the man chiefly concerned in the murder, stung by an awakened conscience, made a public confession of his share in the deed, wholly exonerating me from any knowledge of his intention. I have borne with what patience I might the taunts of enemies, and the coldness of some who once were friends; but it is pleasant for me, I confess, to be able to assert to you my innocence of a deed from which my whole soul revolts, though all who knew the lord of Gowrie must feel that his doom was richly merited."

"I never believed you guilty," I replied, "even in that terrible moment when I first heard the accusation. I felt then that the thing was impossible, though I could not say why, and the conviction has deepened ever since."

"This generous confidence is like you," he said in a tone of deep feeling; "but it is not on that account the less dear and precious to me. A few of my friends, among whom are the members of your own family, have steadily adhered to me, and their affection has been the one star shining through this long night of darkness and desolation."

I was about to answer, when the entrance of Robert changed the conversation, and our guest soon took his leave.

But he came again and again, revealng at each visit so many noble traits, that I knew not which most to admire in him, the hero, the patriot, or the Christian. Time flew swiftly in such society, and before I was aware, my leave of absence had expired, and I was obliged to tear myself away from a scene endeared to me by every sweet association, to return to one in which there was no congenial element. Still, duty bade me go, and I dared not disobey the call.

But a few days before leaving Lindisfarn, I learned a fact, the knowledge of which has made music in my soul ever since. I learned that the noble heart, whose value became every day more apparent, was in truth, spite of my weakness and unworthiness, all my own. How this was told me I cannot repeat even on paper. That interview is among the choicest treasures of memory, and never will it be unveiled for the inspection of mortal eyes. It is enough to say that my whole heart responded to his words, and with the frankness he merited I told him so.

But alas, how transient are all earthly enjoyments. Hardly had I begun to realize my newly found happiness, when the cup was dashed from my lips by the remembrance that a long and bitter separation was before us, during which my hero would be constantly exposed to danger and death, and that I could do nothing to avert it. But Colonel Lyndsay would not suffer me to dwell on this view of the subject.

"You have given me," he said, "a new and strong motive for the preservation of a life hitherto of small value to me; and never forget, my Kathie, that the same kind and powerful Preserver who watches over you here, is also with me in the tented field and amid the roar of battle. Let the name, MIZPAH, Gen. 31:49, be a sign and watchword between us, when we are parted one from the other, and then, whatever may be the will of God concerning us on earth, our hearts can never again be disunited."

He is gone, and I am alone; yet not alone, for a loved presence seems ever near me, and my heart grows strong in the sweet companionship. To-morrow I go back to Edinburgh, where I must remain for the present, as the queen refuses to give me up; and at this time, when dark clouds are gathering round her, I am unwilling to tear myself away. Two happy days I spent at Hope Castle with Colonel Lyndsay, Robert, and Veronica, and the recollection will go with me to Holyrood to cheer me in the hours of loneliness that must inevitably be my lot.

XXV.

A Night of Horror.

"Still as the lip that's closed in death,
Each gazer's bosom held his breath;
But yet afar from man to man,
A cold, electric shiver ran,
As down the deadly blow descended
On him whose hopes and life thus ended."

MARCH 6, 1566.

SINCE my return to Holyrood there has been little to record save scenes of trouble and confusion constantly succeeding each other in the palace. From the hour of her ill-omened marriage, the poor queen has been in the midst of plots and counterplots; so that she has had little time for rest or peace. Even her husband, on whom she has conferred the title of king, and who owes so much to her goodness, treats her with marked discourtesy and even rudeness, and loses no chance of allying himself with her avowed enemies. The earl of Murray, loved and trusted by the queen above all other subjects, raised the standard of rebellion against his sister and sovereign on various pretenses, and she was actually obliged to take the field in person before he could be put down

A few days after leaving Edinburgh, she found herself at the head of eighteen thousand troops, among whom was the regiment commanded by Major Munroe, the husband of my sister Jessie. This loyal subject and brave soldier, finding his patron, the earl of Murray, in arms against his sovereign, refused to follow him to the field on such an errand, declaring that, as none of his ancestors had ever been traitors, he would not be the first to transmit to his son a name thus stained with dishonor.

The rebels fled before the forces of

Queen Mary and Lord Darnley, and the leaders—the Lord Murray, the earl of Glencairn, and others—were banished from the kingdom, and fled for refuge to England, where, it is strongly suspected, Elizabeth is only too ready to receive and protect them. Deprived thus of her counsellors, our royal mistress was compelled to trust more than she had ever done before to her private secretary, David Rizzio, whom, though a foreigner and a rigid Catholic, I believe to be an honest man and truly devoted to the queen's service.

The lords of the Privy Council, who remain at court, Morton, Ruthven, and others, become every day more stern and gloomy; and it is apparent to me and others, though her majesty seems ignorant of it, that the king is far more in the confidence and intimacy of these noblemen than is consistent with his fidelity to his wife and queen. Indeed I must say, even at the risk of failing in becoming reverence, that this young lord, though the consort of a queen, is little more than a tool in the hands of the factious noblemen who are troubling and defying their royal and liege lady. All the love she lavishes upon him is apparently thrown away, or only adds to the arrogance and self-conceit of this infatuated nobleman.

Wearied and sick at heart as I am in this abode of strife and intrigue, nothing but the assurance of my mistress that my presence and sympathy are a comfort to her in the strait to which she is reduced, would detain me in Edinburgh for an hour. When I think of Hope Castle and Lindisfarn, with the peace and quiet constantly brooding over those blessed homes, I long for the wings of a dove, that I might fly away and be at rest.

Twice only, since the happy weeks spent with Veronica last fall, have letters come to me from the far-off friend whose presence helped to make them so delightful. He is still with the prince, beset with cares and duties, yet hopeful and cheerful, with a heart tender and warm as ever yet beat beneath the warrior's coat of mail. When my spirit seems cold and dead to every thing besides, I can always thank God for having given me the rich treasure of an interest in that true and noble heart. Even if we are parted for ever on earth, as I sometimes fear, sure I am that. having once met and mingled like kindred drops, our souls will be for ever united in that better land which remaineth for those who love and serve the Redeemer faithfully on earth.

16th.

The fears and misgivings mentioned in my last have been too soon and fatally realized. The bolt has fallen; but though the first victim is only a helpless foreigner, the hunters had in view a far nobler quarry, and our poor queen is now caught in the toils and held as a captive, guarded and watched by the Argus eyes of jealous tyranny. Ever since the evening of the 9th, that night of horrors, her intellect, usually so clear and bright, seems at times almost unsettled, and the few personal attendants allowed her by her jailors find it extremely difficult at such seasons to soothe and restrain her. Of all her maids of honor, I alone have been permitted to remain with my royal mistress through these days and nights of anguish and despair. This exception in my favor is owing to the high standing of my father and uncle among the Protestant lords, who are just now anxious to secure their favor in the lawless steps that have been taken against their sovereign. But though my friends are devoted heart and soul to the reformation, and though they lament the imprudent steps taken by her majesty, still they would never by word or deed sanction any act of rebellion against her authority.

Before this can reach her, my friend will undoubtedly have heard of the events now transpiring here; still, I will endeavor, so far as I can recall those fearful scenes, to relate the occurrences that have taken place.

The night of the 9th (that fatal night!) was dark and dismal as the deed it sheltered with its protecting wing. There was a drizzling rain constantly falling, which banished every human being from the streets, and an unwonted air of solitude pervaded the grim and dusky edifices which towered to the height of ten or twe've stories against the gray horizon. But while the streets were thus deserted, save where some tall figure, whose clanging step told that he was armed cap-à-pie, stole along with his fellow conspirators to take possession of all the avenues leading to Holyrood, within the palace all was light and cheerfulness. In a small cabinet, not more than twelve feet in width, which communicates with the queen's chamber, the board was spread for her majesty, glittering with gold and crystal, and covered with the delicacies of the evening meal.

Our royal mistress, having thrown by her robes of state, was attired in the elegant simplicity of a private lady, and sat there joyously conversing with the few whom she had selected as most worthy of her special favor. Besides her four Maries and myself there were only the countess of Argyle, the beautiful and brilliant natural sister of the queen, and her secretary, Master Rizzio, who had been invited to share the privacy of her majesty

Deprived as she was of the care and attention of her husband, who seemed to prefer the society of the rough, untutored barons of the court to that of his lovely wife, she found in the companionship of the accomplished Italian, who had never yet presumed upon her goodness, some solace for the neglect of Lord Darnley. The favor with which she regarded him may have been imprudent, but surely it was innocent and pardonable in one so situated.

The countess was in high spirits, and uttered many a gay jest, but the secretary, contrary to his usual wont, was sombre and even sad, and when he answered to the raillery of the countess or of the queen, his tones were grave and melancholy, as if the shadow of approaching doom were even then upon him.

"What has happened to our worthy secretary?" at length the queen inquired, after many vain attempts to turn the current of his thoughts. "Thou art as unlike the gay and gallant Signor Rizzio of other days as thou art to the stern and steel-clad men who throng our court, and even intrude on our privacy."

It seemed as if her words conjured up an apparition, for at that moment the door communicating with her private chamber was rudely opened, and a tall figure, clad in steel from head to foot, entered the cabinet. A loud shriek from some of the terrified women drew the attention of her majesty, who sat with her back to the door, to the intruder. Master David, pallid with terror, gazed intently on the scowling baron, in whom he recognized one of his deadliest foes.

"Rise, unworthy minion," came in hollow accents from the lips of Lord Ruthven, "rise and leave this presence, to which thou art a foul blot and plague-spot. Thine hour is come."

"Lord Patrick Ruthven if mine eyes deceive me not," at length said the queen in measured accents; "what means, my lord, this insolent intrusion?"

Lord Darnley, who had now entered, followed by his base associates, Ker, Douglas, and Balantyne, answered roughly,

"It means, madam, that our patience is exhausted, and that the race of your base minion is well nigh run."

"Comes the blow from thee, Darnley? In sooth I might have surmised this before. What is the pleasure of your grace?"

"My pleasure is, madam, that yonder base Italian, the destroyer of my honor and yours, shall die. Had he a thousand lives, they would hardly suffice for my vengeance."

"Never, Henry Darnley, never! my own life sooner." She stood before him fearless and flashing with indignation, as she went on: "Dost thou think to put a stain like this on the honor of a loyal wife and a crowned queen? Out upon thee for a heartless, cowardly assassin! Leave me now, and I will forgive thee all, even this last outrage. Take hence these thy ruffianly associates; spare an honest man and faithful servant, one who never, never wronged thee even in thought, and I will take thee again to my heart, and love thee as I have ever loved thee, even when most cruel.

Oh, hear me, Darnley, my husband, hear me."

The weak king was evidently moved; his lips quivered, and if left to himself all might still have been averted; but the fierce Ruthven feared the result of the queen's appeal, and cried out,

"Away with this foolish dalliance; we but lose time. On, gentlemen, and drag the fellow from this presence."

As he spoke, he strode forward himself to set the example to his followers; but the terrified secretary, shrieking for mercy, clung to the robe of his beloved mistress, who still stood between him and his foes.

"Mercy," she cried aloud, "mercy for an innocent and unarmed man! As ye hope for mercy in your sorest need, so grant it to him now. Oh that I had been born a man, ye then should rue this deed; aye, and ye shall rue it now!"

I cannot describe the scene that followed this unheeded cry for mercy. There is in my mind a confused recollection of the queen herself struggling with the murderers; of a blow aimed at Rizzio over her shoulder; of his being dragged from the room into the bedchamber of the queen, where the bloody work was completed, fifty-six wounds having been given to the unfortunate victim by the infuriated ruffians.

When all was over, Ruthven strode back into the cabinet, and seating himself, called for a glass of wine, saying that recent sickness had made him weaker than his wont. Her majesty had been weeping violently, but at this last insult she dried her eyes, exclaiming:

"Never again will I demean myself to pray for mercy from butchers. Tears are for those who can do nothing else.

For me, I have henceforth one duty in life, and it shall be mine end, mine aim, my study, and my prayer, to be avenged."

But though the unhappy Rizzio was beyond the reach of his enemies, their work was only just begun. On attempting to leave the room after the departure of the murderers, we found ourselves close prisoners in the two apartments communicating with each other. In vain our royal mistress called and even shouted for her guards; all was silent; and we learned only too soon that the palace was filled with the retainers of Ruthven and others to the number of five hundred. That very night, by some strange understanding, the banished lords, Murray and his friends, came back from England; and orders were issued from the Privy Council in the name of the queen, in order to deceive the populace by whom she was greatly beloved.

Even now, when it is over, my heart sinks within me as I look back on those long days and nights of suffering, uncheered by even one ray of hope, during which the queen, Lady Fleming, and myself were alone, with one faithful female servant whom neither bribes nor threats could induce to forsake her mistress. It was then I saw, as I had never seen it before, the powerlessness of the Romish faith to sustain those who trust it in the hour of suffering and sorrow. The poor queen passed constantly from the extreme of burning indignation to that of utter despair; and even when prostrate before the crucifix, seemed to find no help nor comfort from the prayers offered there. Once when I ventured to say, as she was weeping bitterly,

"Dear lady, look up; God has not forsaken the earth, and he can give your grace help and deliverance if you will only trust in him," she answered me so sadly,

"Oh, my Kate, I know not the Being of whom you speak. He is very far off, while my enemies are near, and powerful as they are merciless. Holy mother of God have pity upon me."

Oh how I longed to be able to lead my dear mistress to that blessed source of comfort and strength which had so recently been revealed to my own soul. When I contrasted her restless agony with the calm and sweet submission of my dear mother and sister in that dark hour when the life of a husband and father was trembling in the balance, how fervently I thanked God for the faith which can thus rob sorrow and death of their sting.

After three or four days of close captivity, the queen managed, through her servant, to convey a message to Lord Darnley, which soon brought that noble man to her apartment. She could always, when alone with him, exert a powerful influence over his feelings, for her mind and will are far stronger than his; and in this interview she made him feel how unwise he had been in separating his interests from hers, who alone could give him influence or power in the realm. She told him plainly that he was but a puppet in the hands of unscrupulous men, who as soon as their purposes were gained by his assistance, would throw him aside without a moment's hesitation. Darnley has a heart, though it is sadly warped and perverted; and here was a young and lovely woman, his wife as well as his sovereign, about to become a mother, and pleading with eloquent tears as well as words for a recon ciliation which it was his interest to grant. The result may be easily imagined. Harmony was once more restored, and a plan arranged by which the royal Mary hoped that very night to gain her freedom.

The attempt was successful, and the queen, with Lord Darnley and two attendants, escaped from the palace and rode on horseback to Dunbar without drawing rein. There they were joined by several noblemen with their retainers, and before leaving Dunbar the earl of Murray and the other banished lords came to the camp, and making due acknowledgments, were taken into favor, and returned to Edinburgh in her train Ruthven and his brutal associates, finding themselves thus forsaken by Darnley, Murray, and the rest, fled at once to England, taking the places so lately vacated by the rebel earls.

In little more than a week from the time of her departure by stealth and in the night, the queen returned in triumph to Holyrood, once more freed from the robber band with which it had been infested. All now seems quiet, but no one can wonder that I feel constantly as if walking over a mine which may at any time explode, and bury the court under its ruins.

XXVI.

The Handwriting on the Wall.

"God hath numbered thy kingdom, and finished it."
"Thou art weighed in the balances, and art found wanting."

Oct. 30, 1566.

FOR a few months after the return of the court to Edinburgh, there was apparent amity between the king and his royal consort; things went on as usual, and poor Rizzio seemed forgotten, though since his death the queen has never been quite like herself. She is moody, changeful, and capricious; sometimes in extravagant spirits, then without cause sunk in the deepest melancholy. The earl of Murray is more attentive than ever, kind and affectionate in manner;

and even that stern reformer Knox has recently spoken of the queen with more sympathy and respect than ever before.

I have seen much of him and his good wife within the year past, for the troubles of her majesty have rendered her more thoughtful of those about her, and more willing to make them happy in their own way. Not long since, as I was preparing to attend her to chapel, she said to me pleasantly,

"Nay, Kate, I know thy heart is elsewhere, and in the name of the Virgin, go where it liketh thee best. God forbid that Mary Stuart should cause a heart that loves her to ache, or even to hunger for that which is in her power to bestow. If, as I surmise, thou wilt hear Master Knox hold forth, tell us on thy return how he now stands affected towards the throne."

With this permission, I lost no time

in availing myself of the privilege, and since then have attended the preaching of the good man almost constantly. He seldom speaks against the queen's measures in public; for with the instinct of noble minds, he will not even seem to attack a falling enemy, and such he evidently considers my royal mistress. Indeed, he has said to me in private that it was his firm belief that, but for her situation, Mary Stuart would ere this have ceased to reign in Scotland.

"God has laid it upon me," he said once to aunt Margaret and myself, who as women were pitying the hard lot of the queen, "so that I could not give it the go-by, to oppose the idolatrous belief and practices of this Scottish queen with a French heart; but she is a goodly and a grand creature, and but for her mistaken education, might perhaps have filled the throne worthily and with profit to the nation. But an evil training and evil counsellors have been her ruin, and now it is easy to read in the signs of the times her coming doom."

And is it even so? Must this lovely and fascinating woman, because she had the misfortune to be born a queen, see her sun go down, while it is yet morning, in hopeless night? There are many things, besides the prediction of Master Knox, which make me fear and almost believe it.

A new favorite has appeared at court, and is at present all-powerful with her majesty. This is James, Lord Bothwell earl of Orkney, one of the lords who rallied to the royal standard at Dunbar, and since that time has been constantly near the person of his sovereign. This nobleman has glorious gifts of person and manner, which make him like a king among men; but he is vain, haughty, and overbearing, and so utterly selfish, that the interests of others are as nothing when they seem to stand in the way of his own. He treats Lord Darnley with undisguised contempt, and the breach between the royal pair, seemingly healed, has been constantly widening.

Among the lords, Bothwell stands alone, for his excessive pride creates a barrier between him and them ; but the queen scorns to conceal the favor with which she regards him, having just made him keeper of Hermitage Castle and of the Valley of Liddesdale, a section of country full of faction and discontent, and therefore of great importance to the crown.

The birth of a prince in June was an event of great political importance, as it served to draw together more closely the queen's party, and gave to the common people an occasion of unmingled rejoicing. Even Lord Darnley, who for months has been in a kind of disgrace, neglected alike by all parties, once more took his proper place in the palace, and attended the christening of his infant son, which was conducted with all the splendor imaginable.

But this hollow truce was of short duration. Lord Darnley soon retired to his former obscurity, and even determined, like a rash and wayward boy, to leave the kingdom and go back to England. It required all the persuasions and authority of his father, the earl of Lennox, and of the queen, to prevent him from taking a step so disgraceful to both parties.

During the summer the very air was rife with reports and gossip in relation to the new favorite; and the few who still really loved and honored Mary mourned in secret over her imprudent and misplaced confidence. Early in October, Bothwell left Edinburgh for his post at Hermitage Castle, and soon afterwards he received a wound in the arm and hand while attempting to bind an outlawed borderer whom he had himself taken prisoner. On hearing of this accident, the queen went to Hermitage Castle to pay a visit of condolence to the wounded keeper; and though she remained only one day in his company, this ill-timed step subjected her to the most violent and scathing rebukes from all her counsellors.

But one brief hour of sunshine was yet to gild the wearied life of the queen, and strange to say, it had its origin in pain and sickness. Lord Darnley was attacked with small-pox; and loathsome as that disease is, her majesty, who had it in her youth, went to him at once, and in spite of all remonstrance, stayed with him day and night till his recovery. No woman in the humbler walks of life, whose whole soul was given to her husband, could have watched more faithfully and untiringly by his bed of pain than did Mary of Scotland over one who had, ever since their marriage, insulted and outraged her in every possible way as wife, woman, and crowned queen. But unfortunately, with returning health came renewed coldness and alienation, and now the king and his royal consort seldom meet or exchange even a word in greeting.

My situation here becomes so painful that I have resolved to quit it, and return to the quiet home and private life which I have so long coveted in vain. While I could hope by my residence here to contribute in any way to the comfort of my sovereign, it was duty to remain; but that time is now past. No one, not even her favorite Maries, have any abiding influence over her, for she takes counsel only of her impulses and affections, and these are constantly changing. There are times when she is all her own noble, royal self again, and at such times I feel as if I could never leave her; but I need rest, and besides this, next summer I hope to welcome my Flemish hero back to Scotland, and the thought of meeting him here at Holyrood is very painful to me. Jessie and her husband are now in Germany, whither Major Munroe has gone, sick at heart of public life and political intrigues at home.

Sir James Dunbar claims Robert and Veronica as permanent residents at Lindisfarn; and since Max has left Scotland to return no more, he would be lonely indeed without them. But in the mean time my dear parents are left childless in their ancient halls; and though with the freedom from selfishness which marks their character, they leave the question entirely to me, I know and feel that my first duty is at home.

XXVII.

The Kirk of Field.

HOPE CASTLE, NOV., 1567.

IT is all over now. The pomp and pageantry that for six years past have filled the old palace of kings at Holyrood have passed away, and silence and desolation now reign in the halls which so lately echoed to the tread of the young, the gay, and the beautiful. Mary Stuart, the idol of the French court and the anointed queen of her own fair native land, is now a solitary prisoner in the petty castle of Lochleven, with but three or four attendants of all the princely retinue that were wont to follow her footsteps and do her bidding. The fall has been so sudden and so great, that in commiserating her misfortunes one almost forgets her faults; still it cannot be denied that, from the time of her acquaintance with Bothwell, every step taken by her has tended more and more to render the present one inevitable.

While it is impossible for me to believe her an actual accomplice in the murder of her second husband the unfortunate Lord Darnley, still it must be confessed that Bothwell and his tools, who were guilty of the deed, had too much reason to think that Mary would rejoice to be free from her chains, however that liberty might be obtained. Her immediate marriage to the murderer, one of the most unhappy acts of an unhappy life gave full occasion for the slander of her enemies, that her hand was the price of blood. But I will not go over all the sorrowful past, but will endeavor to state briefly the immediate circumstances attending the death of the king on that terrible night of February last.

I forgot to state in my former narrative, that in October, the returned lords, Murray, Glencairn, and others, prevailed upon the queen to recall from exile Morton, Ruthven, and their associates who for the murder of Rizzio had been banished from the realm. Sorely against her will she consented that all, excepting Douglas, who struck the first blow, might be permitted to return. It was an evil hour for her when she did so, for no sooner had they reached Scotland, than Morton united with Bothwell in forming a plan by which to remove Darnley out of their way, after which they hoped to have the queen completely in their power. The attachment of her majesty for the specious but profligate Bothwell rendered it easy for them to carry out their designs, which otherwise they would have found it difficult to do.

Ever since the return of the queen from Jedburgh in January, Lord Darnley had resided by himself in a solitary house at some little distance from the city, called the "Kirk of Field." It was a dismal-looking old building, fit for treason, stratagem, and every evil work; and the unhappy young king—king only in name—spent the tedious hours of convalescence there, deprived of his ordinary sources of enjoyment, and compelled to endure the worst of all society to him—his own sad thoughts. Her majesty visited him occasionally, and spent several days and nights at the house, though she did not attempt to conceal the reluctance with which she went there.

Meanwhile, Bothwell and Morton had

matured their project, and only waited for a suitable opportunity to carry it into effect. This was soon furnished them.

The marriage of Sebastian, one of the court chamberlains, was to be celebrated at Holyrood with all the splendor which Mary loved so well to exhibit, and the rank and beauty of Edinburgh were gathered within the palace to do honor to the invitation of their queen.

Like the night of Rizzio's murder, it was wild and tempestuous without, the west wind rising and sinking in melancholy cadences, now howling fiercely as it shook and rattled the casements, now lulling into a small, shrill murmur, dying away upon the ear. The whole vault of heaven was wrapt in blackness so dense, that, like that of Egypt, it might almost be felt.

But within the palace the guests

recked little of the storm and darkness, for all was light and gayety and brilliance, and never had the beauty and grace of Mary of Scotland been more effective than on this the last night of happiness she was ever to know on earth. When the company of gay masquers had passed through the hall in gorgeous procession, the room was cleared for dancing, the wedding posset was passed round, and brimming cups emptied to the "health of Sebastian and his bride." Then scores of youthful couples rose to lead the branle ; and the fair bride, timidly coming up to her royal mistress, requested as a special act of favor that her grace would honor her by joining in the dance which none could lead so gracefully.

Never in her whole life could Mary refuse a request urged by one she loved ; and this trait in her character gave rise to some of her most imprudent acts. On this occasion she paused for a single moment, and at that moment Bothwell, with a smile of triumph curling his proud lip, advanced, and on bended knee begged her to make the humblest of her servants happy by yielding to him her fair hand for one short dance.

The boon was granted with a smile of princely condescension, and the haughty nobleman led forth his beautiful partner amid suppressed murmurs of admiration from the whole assembly. With an indefinite feeling of anxiety for which I could not account, I watched my royal mistress as she walked through the measures of our national dance, and I saw with terror that the soft words he was whispering in her ear were received with blushes and smiles which might well have encouraged a more timid wooer. His words were of course inaudible to me, but from the expressive gestures and the play of features on both sides, I felt sure that this bold bad man was daring to make love to his queen, and she a wedded wife, in the crowded halls of her own palace, and worse still, that she was listening with patience, if not with too evident pleasure.

But suddenly she started, stopped short in her place, and while face, neck, and brow were flushed even to crimson, she called out in shrill tones,

"What ho! A guard there, a guard for my lord of Bothwell."

At that thrilling cry a hundred swords flashed from their scabbards as their owners crowded round the queen, while Morton and Murray spoke in low tones to her majesty, urging the immediate arrest of Bothwell, and the gray-haired earl of Lennox stood leaning on his rapier, his eyes darting defiance on the man who had dared to rival his unhappy son. In the midst of this commotion the guilty earl stood firm and unmoved, pale indeed, but calm, as if surrounded only by friends, with an air of cool defiance on his broad forehead, and his eyes still fixed in undisguised admiration on the queen.

Just at this moment a deep and sullen roar, as if from an earthquake, burst upon the ears of the crowd, followed by a shock like that of some mighty tower falling from its base, which shook the casements, stunning the ears of all who heard it.

"Good heavens!" shouted Murray; "what means that din? Treason, my lords, base treason. Let no one leave the hall; look to her majesty, and secure the traitor. Fleming, Maitland, see that the trumpets sound to horse. Hark!" Then listening for a moment, he added in his deepest tones, "the populace are rising," as the deep swell of voices without announced the presence of a mighty multitude.

The scene at that moment was one of dire confusion and dismay. The vaulted arches of Holyrood echoed with the clangor of trumpets, the tread of armed men, the tramp of horses, and the hoarse cries of the barons shouting to their followers, while at the upper end of the hall the queen's ladies were gathered about her, crowded together like a company of song-birds who see the hawk about to descend upon them.

I was hastening to join them, when, on passing the spot where the earl of Murray stood, I saw him lay his hand heavily on the shoulder of Bothwell as he said,

"Yield thee, my lord of Bothwell, yield thee; for thou passest not from this presence till these strange events are explained; and if there is guilt, by the bones of my fathers, it shall be fearfully avenged."

The touch of Murray roused Bothwell to madness.

"Thou liest, proud lord," he exclaimed aloud; "if thou dost dare to couple the name of Bothwell with guilt, I tell thee thou liest. Off with thy hold, or perish."

Instantly swords were drawn, and in another moment the two would have been engaged in deadly combat, but, as they were about to close, the loud cry was heard,

"Help! her grace the queen is dying."

Murray put up his sword, and turning quickly, made his way to the spot where the queen lay in a swoon that did indeed resemble death.

"Back!" he shouted to the lords and

others who were crowding round the couch; "would ye gaze upon your queen in her extremity, as if she were only some peasant wench? Call her mediciner hither; he professeth some skill, and it shall go hard with him if he exert it not in her behalf. What ails thee, man?" he added, as a terrified looking attendant entered and stood before him trying to speak, but evidently unable to control his voice.

"The king, the king," he at length faltered, more terrified by the scene before him than by that which he had just left.

"What of the king? Fool, canst thou not speak plainly; tell us, what of Henry Darnley?"

"Murdered, your highness, basely, foully murdered," said another who had entered the room while the earl was speaking.

"Nay, not so; the tale has been put into thy mouth," replied Murray, pale with horror.

"He speaks truth, Murray," whispered Morton, who came up at that moment; "Darnley is most cruelly murdered."

"That villain Bothwell! I felt his guilt before I knew it; but he shall rue the deed. Speak out, my lord of Morton; let us know the truth of this accursed deed; and you, ladies, attend your mistress."

Mary, who had come to herself and was sitting on the couch with dishevelled hair and face pale as the dead, gazed on Morton with eyes that seemed starting from their sockets with horror as he told the fearful tale.

"I saw it," he said; "these eyes saw the cold, mangled body cast like that of a worn-out animal on the garden path, the Kirk of Field meanwhile a pile of smoking ruins, blown up with gunpowder, in order to cover this vile treason. There, like a murrained sheep thrown away to rot, lay all that remained of Henry Darnley."

I cannot record the wild and desperate words spoken by the queen as she started from the couch in the frenzy of excitement at this dreadful news. She called upon Bothwell, Rizzio, and Darnley, to come and help her, ordering her grooms instantly to saddle Rosabelle, her favorite palfrey, that she might take horse to avenge her lord and husband. In vain her brother sought to soothe and comfort her, in vain he tried to explain away her words, so that the hungry ears on which they fell might not carry away a conviction of her guilt. Morton shook his head, muttering,

"Sorrow takes not on so wildly. This

savors to my mind of guilt, conscious guilt. Believe it or not, Murray, there is something more here than womanly distraction."

"For my life I would not believe it," Murray replied, "nor must thou, if Morton and Murray are to be still friends. But there is much to do ; come with me to the city-hall, where the Privy Council will soon assemble."

Of the scenes that followed that eventful night I must speak very briefly. Bothwell had a mock trial, and was formally acquitted of the murder of the king, though all present knew that he himself stored the gunpowder, laid the train, and sent a creature of his own to fire it at the proper moment. Not long after this he took forcible possession of the queen's person, and the people were surprised and horror-struck by the announcement that the royal widow had given her hand to the murderer of her husband.

Then came the battle of Carberry Hill, in which Mary and Bothwell, with the few who adhered to their fortunes, met a large body of troops under the command of Morton and other Protestant lords, and suffered a total defeat. Bothwell fled, and was banished to Norway, while the hapless queen, taken captive by her subjects, was deposed, (her infant son being declared king in her stead,) and sent a prisoner to Lochleven Castle, where she still remains.

I took a final leave of her majesty at Holyrood when she was leaving to join Bothwell at Dunbar, and have never seen her since. Tears of pity and regret fill my eyes as I write, for the richest gifts of Providence were showered upon this unfortunate princess, only, it would seem, to make her fall the more signal and complete. With religious principle to guide and strengthen her, what might she not have become? But under the influence of the priests, those "blind leaders of the blind," she has stumbled and fallen, I fear never again to rise.

The earl of Murray, who went to England and France soon after the death of the king, has been recalled and placed at the head of the government, and the influence of Master Knox is all-powerful with him and the other lords of the Privy Council, who justly look upon the great preacher as one of the pillars of the state. The poor little prince, deprived of maternal love and care, is now at Craigmillar Castle, in good health, it is said, and growing rapidly. Poor child! He has been cradled amid scenes of violence and blood, and now deprived of both parents, he is left to the care of strangers. The poorest infant in the kingdom, whose slumbers are watched by a mother's love and guarded by the strong arm of a father, is happier than he on whose baby brows rests a diadem. Master Knox and Dame Margaret have been here on a long visit, and I have learned to love and honor the great reformer as I once never thought to do. I see in him a man raised up by God for a special purpose, with a firmness and persistency which fit him admirably for the work to which he is called, though to his enemies they seem but blind obstinacy. He goes very soon to England and Holland, leaving Aunt Margaret with us; and if, as I still hope, Colonel Lyndsay visits Scotland before spring, they may return in company. The time seems very long since that sad parting at Lindisfarn.

XXVIII.

The Flight and Captivity of the Queen.

"The friends who in our sunshine live,
When winter comes, are flown;
And she who has but tears to give
Must weep those tears alone."

HOPE CASTLE, DEC., 1658.

THE inquiry is very naturally made, How could it happen that a queen should be deprived of her crown and actually put in close confinement by her own subjects, without any form of trial, or even any public accusation against her? It is indeed a strange and unheard-of proceeding, and in any country but Scotland would perhaps be impossible. But here, unhappily, "might makes right;" and the plot against the liberty of the queen had been long maturing, and was too carefully laid to be easily avoided. Morton and his associates, and I fear Murray also, much as they hated Bothwell, were glad to use him as an instrument in the destruction of Mary, who, led on by a fatal affection, fell blindly into the snare laid for her.

If, as I still hope and almost believe, she was innocent of any actual share in the murder of Darnley, I fear she must be held guilty of having connived at it so far as to listen with patience, if not with satisfaction, to the threats of Bothwell on the subject. Then too, her rash and degrading marriage with one whom she must have known to be stained with a fearful crime—all this weighed heavily against her in the public mind, and made it far more easy for the rebellious barons to dethrone her and make the infant James king in her stead.

Still the common people loved their beautiful Mary very dearly, and if she could once have been suffered to appeal personally to them, her doom might still longer have been averted. But Murray and Morton were too wise to run the risk of this step, and she was kept in strict confinement, spite of a solemn promise to the contrary given her by Kircaldy of Grainge, when she surrendered herself after the battle of Carberry Hill.

All Europe has been ringing with the news of her escape from the Castle of Lochleven, through the devotion which she always inspired in all who approached her; of her brief sovereignty, lasting little more than a week; of the battle of Langside, between her troops and those of Murray, her treacherous brother; of her total defeat and subsequent flight to England, where, in an evil hour, she gave herself up into the hands of her enemies.

Elizabeth was not noble or high-minded enough to treat her fallen sister-queen with the respect due to her rank and her misfortunes. She only felt that the rival whom for years she had both feared and hated was now in her power, and in spite of the dictates of good feeling and policy, she resolved on holding her in such strict confinement that escape would be impossible. After the cruel mockery of a trial at York, in which a brother came forward to accuse his sister of profligacy and murder, a trial in which, though they failed to convict her of crime, she was made to feel the worst results of conviction, she was immured in the castle of Tutbury, where she still remains.

Oh, if the unfortunate Mary had but listened to her faithful and loyal Herries, how different might her lot even now have been This nobleman was with her in the hurried flight to his border, constantly entreating her to return and appeal to her people, who had never been wholly estranged from their queen, and would gladly rally round her standard uow that Bothwell was banished from the kingdom. Even at the last moment, when she was about to step into the barge that was to convey her from her own rebellious realm to free and happy England, Lord Herries bent the knee for the last time to his beloved mistress, exclaiming,

"Hear me, Oh, hear me, my noble liege, when on bended knee I entreat you to pause while yet you may. For years has Herries been your faithful servant in the council and the field, with ready hand and true word, ever ready to serve the Stuart."

"Ever, ever true and loyal," replied Mary with a burst of tears; "thou art my noble Herries; and bitter, most bitter has been the reward of truth and valor; but so it has ever been with Mary. I tell thee, baron, for me to love a bird, a tree, or a flower, was always fatal to it; and even affection true and devoted as thine shares the common fate; all whom I loved I have destroyed. The arm of the stoutest warrior lost its might in Mary's service. Alas, for the brave spirits, whose forms, once so nobly filled, are now food for ravens on that dark battle-field!"

"Think not, speak not of them, royal lady; shed not one tear for them. They died right nobly and valiantly, in defence of the fairest cause that ever hallowed the blade of a soldier. They are at rest, and feel no longer their country's woes; but Oh, think of those who would freely give their hearts' best blood to see thee once more free and in safety. Oh, hear me, royal Mary, my queen and mistress, for the first and last time, hear the prayer of Herries. Elizabeth, crafty and cruel, hath ever hated thee, and now thou art about to trust thyself in her power. Go not, I pray thee, as thou lovest name, fame, or liberty, go not to this accursed England."

Even this pathetic appeal was in vain. With that obstinacy which, in the crisis of their fate, seems always to have possessed the Stuarts, Mary refused to listen to her faithful servant, and went forward to a fate worse than death.

This devoted friend, Lord Herries, and the old duke of Chatelherault, almost the only two who dared publicly to adhere to the queen's cause, were arrested by order of the Council, and imprisoned in the castle of Edinburgh.

In justice to the regent Murray, I ought to say that, since his accession to power, his course has been such as to win the confidence and respect of all parties. He has steadily carried forward the work of reformation ; and Master Knox, who is his warm friend and counsellor in all matters relating to the church, believes him earnest and sincere in his religious opinions.

For myself, I cannot yet acquit him of double-dealing towards his too confiding sister and queen; for she loved and trusted him with all her heart, and a word from him had more effect upon her than the prayers and entreaties of others. But though Murray is the one who has profited most by Mary's fall, Master Knox declares that Murray knew nothing of the dark and treacherous designs which led to that event, but even to the last wished and sought to save her. He had one parting interview with the captive queen, in which he reproached her with severity for the acts of folly and imprudence of which she had been guilty. The queen was greatly incensed, and on her part, charged him with treachery in betraying the love and confidence she had always shown him, and using her influence, as she verily believed, for the advancement of his own selfish purposes. This was indignantly denied by Murray, and the brother and sister parted in anger, perhaps never again to meet on earth.

Veronica and Jessie, with their husbands and children, are now at the castle, and it is delightful to hear the pattering of little feet and the sound of sweet, childish voices ringing through the galleries and chambers of this old home. It is more than half a century since these apartments have been graced with similar visitants, and Veronica pleases us by imagining the amazement felt by these ancient echoes when they find themselves repeating such unwonted sounds.

Robert is very proud of his boy, who is my dear father's namesake; and though delicate in person and features, little Alick is a noble child, with thoughtfulness and sensibility far beyond his years.

Veronica, though a happy and devoted mother, is not, I am glad to say, so entirely absorbed in her boy as to be capable of attending to nothing else. She is just as pleasant and genial a companion as before; and even a childish scream from Alick has no power to disturb her equanimity when she knows him to be in good hands, even if they are not her own. Her schools, her clubs for the poor, all the objects of her care and attention, seem just as interesting to her now as before this new claimant on her time made his appearance.

One day when I was expressing what I felt on this subject, she replied with a smile,

"I know what you mean, dear Kathie, and have often felt annoyed by the exclusive devotion of which you speak. I believe that, next to God, the first duties of a wife and mother are to her husband and children; but the difficulty is, that some young mothers make not only the first, but the second, third, and fourth, and indeed all their duties begin and end there. We were daughters, sisters, and members of society before we were mothers or wives, and some of the duties owing in those relations must continue to be binding upon us; for I am sure God never made our obligations to clash with each other. It seems to me very much like refined selfishness to suffer all our care and interest to centre in one or two objects, simply because they are a part of ourselves, to the exclusion of every other."

"But, Veronica," said Jessie, who was listening attentively, "do you remember that God has committed the souls as well as the bodies of our children to us for safe-keeping? and can we think too much of such a charge?"

"Certainly not, my sister; if we neglect it, we are doubly guilty, and shall be sorely punished for our remissness, either in this world or the next. I said, you will recollect, that a mother's first duty, next to her duty to God, was to her own family; and this includes religious training, guidance, and constant care; but as you look through society, do you find that the mothers who never have a thought or feeling beyond the nursery are the most careful to train up their children in the nurture and admonition of the Lord? My experience has led me to a very different conclusion."

"Veronica is right," I said; "and if I may be allowed a share in this discussion, I must say I have always noticed that those indulged and petted children who from the cradle are made to believe themselves the centre of the universe, are usually rude, selfish, and disobedient above all others. I have not looked far enough to discover the reason, but the fact must be evident to all."

Jessie sighed; for her own little Hector, a fine, sturdy boy of four, with his father's manliness and courage, is the idol of her heart; and without knowing it, she has suffered him to usurp almost the entire control of her time and thoughts, insomuch that she herself has seemed little more than an enlarged and completed Hector. But this sweet sister is so truly good and desirous of knowing her duty, that I think she will only need to see the right way in order to follow it; and I trust the remarks of Veronica will be of great use to her.

It is now many months since I have heard from Bruges, where Colonel Lyndsay has been residing for the last year. It was impossible for him to come to Scotland at the time appointed, as he had an important command which he could not leave; and since that time, duty has held him fast in spite of his wish to return, if only for a few weeks. I try to be patient and submissive, but the heart will not always echo the sentiment of the lip, "Thy will be done."

When the world is bright before us, and those we love best are at our side, it is easy to trust our heavenly Father's word; but in the dark and stormy day, when earthly props fail us, and our fondest hopes have perished, then nothing but a faith that is divine can enable us to say, "It is the Lord, let him do what seemeth him good."

Hitherto I have known little of sorrow except the name; but the sunny days of youth are almost gone, and something whispers me that the happiness to which I have looked forward with such eager hope will never be mine. But I must not indulge in gloomy forebodings, for I have never found in my Bible that strength is promised us to meet imaginary troubles, but only for the real afflictions that God sends upon us. Sufficient unto the day is the evil thereof.

XXIX.

The Darkened Path.

"But, mortal pleasure, what art thou in truth?
The torrent's smoothness, ere it dash below."

FROM VERONICA TO LADY ELLEN MAXWELL.

HOPE CASTLE, 1569.

IN compliance with the request of my beloved sister, who for months has been and still is unable to write herself, I address you, dear Lady Ellen, for so many years her valued and trusted friend. Our darling Kathie is, I rejoice to say, in better health than when Robert saw you in Paris; but her state of mind is still such as to give us the greatest possible anxiety and distress. Silent and uncomplaining, she moves about the house like a shadow, thoughtful as ever of the happiness of others, but with never a smile on those pallid lips, and no brightness in the tear-dimmed eyes once sparkling with intellect and feeling. It almost breaks our hearts to look upon her, and to feel, as we are forced to do, our utter inability to help or comfort her.

There is but one who can wipe away such tears as hers; and a thick cloud, the effect doubtless of physical prostration, shuts out the Sun of righteousness from her sight. I feel certain that the blessed Saviour is leading her by a safe and sure way, even though it may seem darkened and crooked to mortal eyes; and that ere long the dear mourner will be brought into the light, and enabled from the heart to say, "It is good for me that I have been afflicted."

You expressed a wish to learn the particulars of the sad event which has filled our hearts with sorrow, and not ours only, but the hearts of all who feel that in Colonel Lyndsay Scotland has lost one of her purest and noblest sons. His patriotism was so free from the alloy of selfishness, that wherever he found his fellow-men striving to uphold a good and just cause, his active brain, strong arm, and good sword, were ever at their service; and what that help was worth, let the prince of Orange and his brave companions-in-arms answer.

But with all his strength of intellect, his coolness and courage, and his more than Roman firmness in the defence of truth, he was simple, frank, and genial as a child in the society of those he loved. Alas, that in speaking of one so richly gifted, useful, and beloved, one must employ those sad, sad words so eloquently telling the vanity of earth, *He was.*

You, who know the warm, generous nature of our Kathie, and the readiness with which it responds to every thing grand and beautiful, will not wonder that a character such as I have imperfectly described should find its way at once to her heart, meeting as they did, under circumstances of peculiar interest to both.

Though my sweet sister does not exactly wear her heart upon her sleeve, yet is it so transparent that I, who love her fondly, could read it with ease; and I knew. even before she herself was aware of it, that Norman Lyndsay had secured an interest, little suspected by him, in that guileless heart. After his visit in 1566, when every thing was explained between them, and their troth plighted, her affectiors were given up to him with an intensity that alarmed me; for I know who has said, "Keep yourselves from idols."

It was easy to see that this strong love was drawing her spirit down to earth, and fastening it by a thousand ties fine as the spider's web, yet strong as cable, to the creature instead of the Creator.

Last fall, after an absence of more than two years, Colonel Lyndsay made a flying visit to Scotland; and during the few days of his stay, Kathie's happiness was complete. Her buoyant step, her bright eye and smiling lip, all bore witness to the gladness of her heart. Years seemed to have rolled backward, and she was once more the laughing, joyous Kathie of our early youth. For various reasons, Colonel Lyndsay wished to have the marriage take place before his return, chiefly, I think, to secure beyond the possibility of doubt the estate of Ormistoun to my sister in the event of his death. Kathie thought not of this; she saw one reason alone which to her was all-sufficient; the marriage would give her a right to be at his side if wounded or sick, and for this privilege she would willingly have braved death itself.

But it was not so to be. The ceremony was delayed until the return of our father, Sir Alexander, from Glasgow; and before that time an urgent message from Bruges called Colonel Lyndsay back to that place on business of importance. He went most reluctantly, promising to return as speedily as possible, when Kathie was to accompany him to the Netherlands at her own earnest request.

After his departure, and contrary to her usual habit of anticipating evil, she was in excellent spirits, looking forward with eager delight to the reunion at hand, and forming plans of future happiness too bright to be realized on earth.

How can I tell you the rest? It seems

like stabbing my poor sister again to the heart to write the words that destroyed her earthly happiness at one fatal stroke. A messenger was sent from the prince, bearing a letter written by his own hand, in which, gently and tenderly as such tidings could be imparted, he informed the friends of Colonel Lyndsay of the probable death of that good man and gallant soldier. He was wounded by a sabre stroke, while leading on his troops to sustain the prince, sore pressed by his enemies; and as nothing had been heard from him since, no doubt was entertained of his death, though the body had never yet been found.

Through the mercy of God, Master Knox was at the castle when this letter arrived, and in compliance with our wish, communicated the sad tidings to Kathie. She heard him without reply, apparently stunned by the severity of the blow, and with eyes fixed immovably upon him, sat in stony silence while he endeavored to comfort her by leading her thoughts to God. It was many days before her dry, burning eyeballs were moistened with a tear; and during that time she never spake, except in answer to some inquiry, and then as briefly as possible. In vain our dear mother, Jessie, and myself wept over her and prayed with and for her; she was like a breathing statue, passively enduring our attentions, without one word of acknowledgment or return.

It was the voice of a child that at length roused her from this dreadful apathy. Little Hector Munroe, who is very fond of his aunt, constituting himself her body-guard on all occasions, and who was a special pet with Colonel Lyndsay, had been one day watching her attentively, but without speaking, as she sat in her usual manner, with her eyes widely opened and fixed on vacancy. At length, leaving his play, he went up to her, and taking one of her cold hands in both his own rosy palms, he said with sweet earnestness,

"Auntie, what ails you? Why you look at God so, like Janet at bad man when she angry at him? Turnel"—his name for the colonel—"wont love auntie if you stare so, and be so sober all the time. Turnel tell Hector good folks always happy. He good man; laugh with Hector, Oh, so much; he do n't like naughty folks at all. See what he gave Hector to keep always."

The child held up a small ornament, which had been part of the decoration of some military order, and which Kathie had often seen Colonel Lyndsay wear. As the boy placed it in her hand, the frozen heart was melted, the hidden fountains opened, and tears flowed in torrents from her eyes as she threw her arms about his neck, exclaiming,

"Blessed child, you are nearer heaven than I am. Oh, pray for me to our Father, that he will have mercy upon me."

"Shall I say 'Our Father' for you, poor auntie?" he inquired; then kneeling down by her side, and clasping his little hands, he repeated that sublime prayer with touching pathos, adding at the close,

"Please, our Father, tell Turnel that auntie wont be happy unless he comes back again, and Hector wants to see him ever so much."

The childish voice and the sobs of the weeping Kathie alone broke the stillness of the apartment, as we looked in silent wonder on this affecting scene. The reaction saved her reason; but her physical strength was exhausted, and a long and dangerous illness followed, from which she is only now slowly recovering. Her mind was so clouded most of the time during her sickness, that we could never ascertain the state of her feelings ; and even now that her strength is in a measure restored, it seems impossible for her to speak freely even to me, from whom, until now, she has hardly concealed a thought.

I see, with joy and gratitude to God, that this reserve is gradually wearing away, and feel confident that my precious sister will soon be enabled to perceive the light which even now is shining all about her, though she knows it not. When that happy day arrives, I doubt not that you, Lady Ellen, will be the first to learn it from herself, as I know how fondly her heart clung to you, even through this long night of darkness and desolation.

XXX.

Light at Evening Time.

"Through all life's troublous day
Thou hast sustained me. Thou wilt keep me still;
Though clouds and darkness gather round my way,
And hopes are perished, yet I fear no ill;
It matters little what the path may be,
So that it leads to thee."

ORMISTOUN, 1571.

ONCE more, after an interval of more than two years, I have prepared myself to resume my pen, at least until I can tell my distant friend how naturally my thoughts turn to her with an impulse which I cannot control. Brought as I have been out of the depths of misery and despair by a grace nothing less than infinite, I love to speak of the mercy that has saved me, to those whose experience will enable them to understand it.

The first emotion of joy I had felt since the dreadful event that withered all my earthly prospects, was caused by the intelligence contained in a letter from Lady Ellen Maxwell to Veronica, telling her that the writer had learned to know Jesus Christ as he is freely offered in the gospel, not as he appears through the colored and distorted lens of the Catholic church. When the letter was read in my presence, I said nothing, and they all thought the good news unheeded by me; but deep down in my icebound heart one little ray of light and warmth penetrated even then, and now my whole soul is flooded with it. How sweet it is to feel that this dear friend is now my soul's sister for eternity, that we are no longer separated by differing creeds, but heirs together of the grace of life.

When Robert went to Paris last fall, we hardly dared hope that he would gain access to Lady Ellen, guarded as she has always been by the jealous care of Father Francis from contact with heretics; but a kind Providence prepared the way by sending him away from France at that time; and then by what I should once have called an accident, though now I know it to be God's own hand, Robert was thrown in her way just when she needed his assistance, and was prepared to receive him favorably. Then, too, her meeting with Master Andrew Melville, the man of all I know best fitted to solve the doubts of an inquiring mind and direct it to "the Lamb of God who taketh away the sin of the world." All this chain of events seems to me strange and delightful beyond expression.

She has promised, God willing, to revisit her native land next year, and to spend some time with me here; and I am looking forward with eager interest to that time, though I tremble while I do so, remembering the uncertainty of every earthly prospect.

Last year at this time I was a stone, alive only to a sense of intolerable pain and anguish; now I look back to that part of my life with shame and horror, feeling that my punishment, however severe, was justly deserved for having loved the gift more than the Giver, and for daring to build my hopes of happiness on aught beneath the skies.

Until recently I have never ventured to repeat aloud the beloved name so deeply engraven on my heart; but now, when the barbed arrow has been extracted by divine grace, and only the scar remains, I love to repeat it softly to myself and to hear it on the lips of others.

Hector Munroe, my darling little consoler, talked of the Turnel, as he called him, every day while we were together at Hope Castle, and seemed to imagine that in some strange way he was often near us, for he would ask,

"Will Turnel love me if I do this or that?" when requested to deny himself in any way, and his conduct was always regulated by the answer. At other times he would say,

"Turnel wants me to be a good boy, and obey God and mamma and auntie, and so I will, for I love Turnel with all my heart."

Wee Alick, who, though Veronica's child, has far less imagination than Hector, and is more practical in every way, would look at him with innocent wonder in his large brown eyes, saying softly,

"Where is he, Kyter?"—his name for Hector. "I do n't see him anywhere He is n't in this room, is he?"

"Why, Alick, do n't you know?" was

the almost indignant reply. "Turnel is in heaven, mamma says; but if he has wings, can't he fly right down here to see us if he wants to come? I do n't believe heaven is very far off, either; for if it was, you know, Jesus could n't be here every day and there too; so I'm sure Turnel comes with him, for he loved auntie and all the rest, and he'll not forget to come back, for he said he would n't, and he never told lies."

"But," persisted Alick, "my mamma said he was killed far away, and how then can dead folks remember?"

This question troubled the little pleader for a moment, and his countenance looked sad; but suddenly brightening, he exclaimed,

"Oh, Alick, you're too little; you can't understand; but people do n't die all over; and I'm sure if Turnel was dead ever so much, there'd be something left alive to fly up to heaven and love me and auntie."

Sweet infant preacher! The words dropped like healing balm on my aching heart, and I thanked God who, through the lips of a child, had sent me a message so precious.

The private papers and other articles belonging to Colonel Lyndsay have been sent on from Bruges, and it is the sad though pleasant occupation of many an hour to look over and arrange them. These records of the heart, intended for no eye but that of the All-seeing, tell a tale of nobleness and excellence of which until now the half has not been known to me. Stainless honor, warm affections, moral courage, and ardent piety moulding every thought and feeling, all are still living and breathing here, though the dear hand that traced these lines is mouldering in the dust.

How often I have felt, while reading through blinding tears some expressions of affection never intended for my ear, that I would far rather have only the blessed memory of a love like his, than to be the chosen of any living man on earth.

Ormistoun is left by will to me; and as every wish of his is sacred, I have accepted the trust, and am trying, in dependence on the grace of God, to do my duty here as lady chatelaine of the Hall. Captain Farquhar, who for three years had the management of the estate, was greatly beloved and did much good; but he left some time since, and after his departure every thing went back to the old way, for the want of a directing eye and hand, so that I find plenty of occupation for both mind and body. It is soothing to reflect, when weary and almost discouraged, that I am carrying out the last request of my beloved, and that if enabled to do my duty here, a nobler monument will thus be erected to his memory than obelisk or pillar of sculptured marble.

Major Munroe and Jessie are now at Hope Castle, and will remain there permanently, and Robert and Veronica always spend a part of the year there, so that my dear parents will not be left alone; and my father thought with me that my duty was at Ormistoun.

Veronica and little Alick have been with me for some weeks, and my knight Hector is often here, so that I have little time for loneliness, even if I were so disposed. But next to trust in God, I find constant occupation the best possible remedy for sad thoughts; and in the care of my tenantry and the supervision of the schools, together with the necessary attention to guests, of whom there are usually several staying at the Hall I find little leisure for depressing recollections.

Master Knox, who takes great interest in my occupations, and has proved himself one of the kindest and most sympathizing of friends, is now with us, and coming from Edinburgh here, brought us the sad tidings of the death of the regent Murray. He was basely murdered while riding through the street at evening; and though during life many feared and suspected him, all Scotland is lamenting his untimely death. Morton has been appointed regent in his stead, but there is nothing in his character to render him popular with the multitude; and whenever he appears abroad, the sullen silence with which he is received must make him feel that his power rests on an insecure foundation.

Master Knox is a sincere mourner for the Lord James, who, whatever may have been his faults towards others, was ever a true and faithful friend to the great reformer.

Dame Margaret tells us that her husband always prays tenderly for the poor captive queen, and has little sympathy with Elizabeth in her cruel treatment of the unfortunate Mary. Alas, for my unhappy mistress! A wife without a husband, a mother without a child, and a queen without a throne, how full of bitterness is her lot.

Mary Seyton, who went with her to England, has returned, and is about to marry the son of Mary's secretary, Maitland of Lethington. Her sad story of the queen's captivity is enough to touch the hardest heart, and I confess it drew tears from my eyes. I have felt so deeply for her since hearing of the rigorous treatment that she is experiencing, that were it not for the duties which bind me to Ormistoun, I would go at once to England and offer to share her fate, in the hope that I might be of some little use or comfort to her. But the number of her attendants is limited by the cruel and jealous Elizabeth, and but for the firmness and spirit of Lady Fleming, who declared to the messenger of the English queen that she would be drawn in quarters before they should tear her from her mistress, this faithful servant would have been sent back with Mary Seyton.

Sir James Melville, one of the oldest and most valued friends of the poor queen, says there is little hope of her release until the infant king is old enough to feel for his mother, and to demand her release in terms that cannot be disregarded. It is a long, long time to wait for such an event, and it seems to me that the proud and sensitive heart of Mary must break with the sickness of hope deferred long ere that time shall arrive.

But Veronica stands by me, bright, warm, and cheering as a sunbeam, and says with one of her radiant smiles,

"Ah, Kathie dear, that will never do. You have chosen a sad subject, and I know very well what the consequence will be. Lay by your pen, and come out with Alick and me into the blessed air and sunshine, and they will tell you quite a different story."

And is this indeed so? Am I in danger of indulging gloomy and depressing thoughts as I look abroad on the misery that overspreads this fair world of God's fashioning? No, I will not, while faith assures me that the coming of the second Adam shall more than repair the ruins of the fall, and that the regenerated earth shall yet bloom with more than the freshness of Eden's first beauty.

Rather let me make the sublime sentiment of the prophet my own, and say with him, "Although the fig tree shall not blossom, neither shall fruit be in the vines; the labor of the olive shall fail, and the fields shall yield no meat; the flock shall be cut off from the fold, and there shall be no herd in the stalls: yet I will rejoice in the Lord, I will joy in the God of my salvation."

HOPE CASTLE, Oct., 1571.

Am I waking, or do I dream? Is it a vision of the night, like those that have mocked me so often, or a blessed reality that Norman Lyndsay, whom for more than two years I have lamented as dead, is still alive, and perhaps even now on his way to Scotland? I cannot, cannot believe it, and yet not for the wealth of worlds would I doubt it even for a moment. How changed is every thing on which I look. The face of nature seems dressed in smiles, and the goodness of God is written on every thing that meets my eye.

Yesterday I was sitting alone, and thinking, as I looked out on the fading landscape, of the bright hopes that had withered before the flowers, when a message was brought from my mother requesting my immediate presence at the Castle. I came hither at once, fearing she might be ill or in trouble; but one glance at her dear face assured me that she had none but pleasant news to communicate.

She told me—what until now I had not known—that my father, some three or four weeks before, had been suddenly called away from home, and had left without informing even her of his business or destination.

Yesterday a letter came from him dated in the Netherlands, and stating the cause of his hurried departure. It seems that a rumor had reached him through a Scottish soldier who had just come from Holland, that, on taking a stronghold long in the possession of the Spaniards, the Flemings had found in the dungeons of the castle a large number of prisoners-of-war, and among them, still living, though weak and emaciated from close confinement, was Colonel Lyndsay, so long mourned as dead by both countries

When this startling report reached him, my father would not speak of it to any one but Robert, fearful of raising hopes only to be disappointed; but he resolved instantly to go on and learn for himself the truth or falsity of the report. As soon as he arrived at Brussels, he had an interview with the Prince of Orange, who chanced to be there, and who not only confirmed the report, but informed my father that Colonel Lyndsay was then at the Hague, and an inmate of his own palace, having become so much reduced by his severe sufferings as to be unable to leave for Scotland, as he wished to do.

When he wrote, my father had not seen the dear invalid, though he intended soon to visit the Hague, but he would not keep back the blessed news from us even for an hour, so he sent a letter immediately on leaving the cabinet of the prince.

My thoughts are all confusion, and I cannot even try to separate and arrange them. At one moment I am full of impatience, and think it impossible for me to wait an hour for the expected meeting;

the next, I weep over the ingratitude and folly of which I have been guilty, and feel that in the bliss of knowing him still among the living, I could patiently endure another year of separation if necessary. Will this wayward heart ever learn the sweet lesson of waiting quietly upon God, and making his will my own?

Hector, whose little heart has been running over with gladness all day, came to me, saying, "Auntie, I thought if I asked God to let Turnel come back and see us, that he would send him, and now you see he has. Are n't you sorry, auntie, that you looked so sober at God, when he just wanted to see Turnel a little while?"

To-day I am the happiest of mortals, with but one wish ungratified, and that one, I trust, by the goodness of God, will soon be mine. A letter reached me this morning from Colonel Lyndsay, written by his own hand, and containing an account of the strange circumstances by which all his friends have been so long deceived in relation to his fate. It seems that while lying insensible from his wound, he was found and taken prisoner by a band of Italian soldiers from the territories of the duchess of Parma, former regent of the Netherlands. By them he was carried from the field and placed in a baggage-cart going to Antwerp; and in this situation must soon have died from neglect and exposure, added to the severity of his wound, but for the humanity of a young subaltern officer who had charge of the detachment of troops that carried him away.

This young man—blessings on his name for the deed—procured a surgeon for the wounded officer, and on giving him up to the commandant of the fortress, made what arrangements he could for the comfort of his prisoner, and only left him when compelled by his duty to return to his regiment.

He had once been a page in the family of the Count d'Egmont, and though now in arms against the Flemings, had never forgotten his obligations to that great man, and for his sake had vowed to show kindness to any prisoners who might fall into his hands. The governor of the castle, though far less generous and humane than the young officer, treated Colonel Lyndsay with some degree of kindness, though he kept him in a confinement so close and rigorous that no one but himself and the turnkey knew of the existence of such a captive. Here two years and a half passed away, long and dreary years to the noble prisoner, believing as he did that those dearest to him were mourning over him as among the dead.

But this is all past, and now he is coming home again, broken indeed in health but hopeful and buoyant in spirit as ever, while I, blessed beyond my deserts in such a task, shall have the privilege of nursing him back to health and strength again. How glad I am that he will find me at Ormistoun, his own pleasant home, soon, I trust, to be *our* home, the dear spot where, heart linked to heart and hand in hand, we may hope to serve God and our fellow-beings here, till called away to our better and more enduring home above.

www.ingramcontent.com/pod-product-compliance
Lightning Source LLC
LaVergne TN
LVHW010151110826
845151LV00002B/481

* 9 7 8 1 4 2 5 5 3 7 8 0 7 *